GOLDEN NUGGETS
OF
THOUGHT

VOLUME I

Compiled

By

EZRA L. MARLER

BOOKCRAFT

SALT LAKE CITY, UTAH

Thought is the Pattern by which the Man is Molded.—E. L. M.

32nd Printing, 1972

Lithographed in U. S. A.
by
Publishers Press

COMPILER'S COMMENT

Thoughts make us what we are. Through the passing years and ages some of the best thoughts of men have been crystalized in words and preserved in compact form as the heritage of all of us. Mental vitamins they are, which add zest to the joy of living. To me they are sweet morsels of thought which I have, with pleasure and profit, included in my daily mental menu. They are so small, so free from dross and so thoroughly genuine, that I have looked upon them as Golden Nuggets of Thought. Hence the title of this brief compilation.

In picking up these Nuggets by the way there has not always been found title attached. In all cases where origin is known, due credit has been given. If there are any cases to the contrary, it is due wholly to oversight or error.

For years I have carried these tiny literary gems in my pocket, written on cards and bits of paper. Besides their exhilarating effect in my own life, they have helped me very materially in the class room and at the pulpit. They have added beauty, force and vigor to the messages I have tried to present. But these fragments were not easily preserved and were difficult to classify. Then came the thought of making them more convenient for my own use, and at once accessible to others. And so was born this little volume.

I am keenly conscious of the criticisms that may be offered. The reader will probably have in mind many fine things which he or she will feel should have been included. As the compilation was being formed, the greatest difficulty was one of selection. There were so many other inspiring things demanding presentation—so many other topics, and such worthy ones, pleading for treatment, that it was difficult indeed to keep them out.

But it was necessary to draw the line. It was not the object to compile a dictionary of quotations nor an extensive anthology. The aim was to bring together as many as might well be, of these Golden Nuggets of Thought in convenient form to be carried about in men's pockets and women's hand-bags. If they are to be at hand where and when wanted, weight and bulk must be avoided. When leisure moments are with you, these Nuggets can be there also; when you are called to speak or teach or preach, they can be at your finger tips and drawn upon to enrich your message and strengthen your appeal. To have included too many of the good things available, would have defeated the purpose motivating this work. The few that have been selected, I hope you will enjoy. —E. L. M.

ADVERSITY AND AFFLICTION

———

When disaster beats around the true men are found
   And cowards are marked with a brand.
They whimper and whine: they cringe and repine,
   At the whip-lash Fate holds in her hand.
The brave men fight on though chasms may yawn
   And midnight's unlit by a star.
How you face defeat in the crises you meet—
   That measures the man that you are.—*Anon.*

My son, despise not the chastening of the Lord;
neither be weary of his correction;
   For whom the Lord loveth he correcteth.
               —*Proverbs* 3: 11, 12.

THE LIGHT OF FAITH

———

When the dark days come and the clouds grow grey
All men must brave them as best they may,
   With never too much repining;
And bravest is he, when the shadows fall,
Who sees in the gloom of his darkened hall
   The light of his faith still shining.

In those lonely days when his heart shall ache
And it seems that soon shall his courage break,
There is only one place to borrow;
One place to go for the strength he needs,
He must bind with faith every wound that bleeds,
And cling to his faith through sorrow.
For truly forlorn is the man who weeps
When his dead lies buried in floral heaps
And friends his path are lining;
And a pitiful creature he's doomed to be
If he cannot look through the gloom and see
The light of his faith still shining.—*Edgar A. Guest*

From Mr. Guest's book *The Light of Faith,* copyright 1926, used by permission of The Reilly & Lee Co., Chicago.

THE REASON WHY

Not 'til the loom is silent
  And the shuttles cease to fly,
Will God unfold the pattern,
  And explain the reason why.
The dark threads were as needful,
  In the weaver's skillful hand,
As the threads of gold and silver,
  In the pattern that he planned.
          —*Unknown.*

The wisdom of God appears in afflictions. By these He separates the sin which He hates from the son whom He loves. By these thorns He keeps him from breaking over into Satan's pleasant pastures, which would fatten him indeed, but only for the slaughter.—*Aughey.*

Affliction is a sort of moral gymnasium in which the disciples of Christ are trained to robust exercise, hardy exertion, and severe conflict.
—*Hannah More.*

Many men owe the grandeur of their lives to tremendous difficulties.—*Spurgeon.*

The fineness and strength essential to our best being, and to make us do our work, come by the hammer and the fire, by the thorn in the flesh, the trouble and pain in our life, which may act in us as the fire acts in the iron, welding the fiber afresh.—*Robert Collyer.*

Thou are never at any time nearer to God than when under tribulation, which he permits for the purification and beautifying of thy soul.—*Molinos.*

THE RAINY DAY

The day is cold and dark and dreary—
It rains, and the wind is never weary.
The vine still clings to the mouldering wall;
But at every gust the dead leaves fall
And the day is dark and dreary.

My life is cold and dark and dreary—
It rains and the wind is never weary.
My thoughts still cling to the mouldering past;
But the hopes of youth fall thick in the blast
And the days are dark and dreary.

Be still, sad heart! and cease repining;
Behind the clouds is the sun still shining.
Thy fate is the common fate of all;
Into each life some rain must fall—
Some days must be dark and dreary.
                    —*Henry Wadsworth Longfellow.*

That person who cannot bear chastening cuts
himself off from the blessings of Heaven.
                    —*Ophelia Kennedy.*

A dose of adversity is often as needful as a
dose of medicine.—*B. C. Forbes.*

If times are hard and you are blue
Think of others worrying too.
Just because your trials are many,
Don't think others haven't any.
Life's made up of smiles and tears,
Joys and sorrows, mixed with fears;
And though to us it seems onesided
Trouble is pretty well divided.
If we could look in every heart,
We'd find that each one has its part
And those who travel fortune's road
Sometimes carry the biggest load.

—*Anonymous.*

Sweet are the uses of adversity;
Which, like the toad, ugly and venomous,
Wears yet a precious jewel in his head.

—*Shakespeare.*

AGE

"Worry, doubt, self-distrust, fear and despair —these are the long, long years that bow the head and turn the growing spirit back to dust."

"Year's wrinkle the skin, but to give up enthusiasm wrinkles the soul."

AGE

Age is a quality of mind:
If your dreams you've left behind,
  If hope is cold,
If you no longer look ahead,
If your ambition's fires are dead,
  Then you are old.

But if from life you take the best,
And if in life you keep the zest,
  If love you hold,
No matter how the years go by,
No matter how the birthdays fly,
  You are not old.

                —*Edw. Tuck.*

Youth is not a time of life—it is a state of mind. It is not a matter of ripe cheeks, red lips and supple knees; it is a temper of the will, a quality of the imagination, a vigor of the emotion; it is a freshness of the deep springs of life. Youth means a temperamental predominance of courage over timidity, of the appetite for adventure over love of ease. This often exists in a man of fifty, more than in a boy of twenty. Nobody grows old by merely living a number of years; people grow old only by deserting their ideals.—*Anonymous.*

GROWING OLD

A little more tired at close of day,
A little less anxious to have our way,
A little less ready to scold and blame,
A little more care for another's name,
And so we are nearing the journey's end,
Where time and eternity meet and blend.

A little less care for bonds and gold,
A little less zest than in days of old,
A broader view and a saner mind,
And a little more love for all mankind,
A little more careful of what we say;
And so we are faring adown the way.

A little more love for the friends of youth,
A little more zeal for established truth,
A little more charity in our views,
A little less thirst for the daily news,
And so we are folding our tents away,
And passing in silence at close of day.

—*Rollin J. Wells.*

"You are as young as your faith, as old as your doubt; as young as your self-confidence, as old as your fear; as young as your hope, as old as your despair."

In the central place of your heart there is a wireless station; so long as it receives messages of beauty, hope, cheer, grandeur, courage and power from the earth, from men and from the Infinite, so long are you young. When the wires are all down and the central place of your heart is covered with the snows of pessimism and the ice of cynicism, then are you grown old, indeed.

—Selected.

If wrinkles must be written upon your brows, let them not be written upon the heart. The spirit should never grow old.—*James A. Garfield.*

ASPIRATIONS

Build thee more stately mansions, O my soul,
    As the swift seasons roll!
Leave thy low-vaulted past!
Let each new temple, nobler than the last,
Shut thee from heaven with a dome more vast,
Till thou at length art free;
Leaving thine outgrown shell by life's unresting
    sea.—*Holmes.*

IMAGINATION AND ENTHUSIASM

Take imagination and enthusiasm,
    And hitch the two together,
Then fix your gaze on the farthest star
    And forget about the weather.

Take a pound of pluck and energy
    And mix with an ounce of thrift,
Then forward-march to the heights ahead,
    And don't be begging à lift.

Pick out the hill you want to climb
    And fix your gaze on the peak,
Then blaze your way to the very top,
    The bottom is reserved for the weak.

Imagination and enthusiasm;
    Mark you! this matchless team,
Is yours to harness and drive to the goal,
    Of all your heart has dreamed.

Imagination and enthusiasm;
    Oh man! if you are wise,
You'll give 'em the rein, then fix your gaze
    On the brightest star in the skies.

                        —*W. C. Thurston.*

So nigh is grandeur to our dust,
   So near is God to man,
When duty whispers low, "I must,"
   The youth replies, "I can."
             —*Emerson.*

UPWARD REACHING

The soul of man, to what end is it striving?
What is the destiny, what is the goal?
This constant upward reaching of the soul—
What force behind it does the ceaseless driving?
Upward reaching but implies a quest
Unending, for the things we deem the best,
For that which goes to make the perfect whole—
Insatiable striving for a better role.

With what speed, then, is man's success arriving?
Endowed with instincts meant to goad him on
Toward the infinite, from dawn to dawn,
From his struggle, how much good deriving?
Man's speed, or progress, toward that holier sphere,
Is measured through the knowledge he gains here,
And man will go on reaching endlessly;
There is no terminal—no finality.
           —*Amelia Peart Macdonald.*

   Do you ask to be the companion of nobles?
Make yourself noble, and you shall be. Do you

long for the conversation of the wise? Learn to understand it, and you shall hear it. But on other terms, no. If you will not rise to us, we can not stoop to you.—*Ruskin.*

Ideals are like the stars—we never reach them, but like the mariners on the sea we chart our course by them.—*Carl Schurg.*

THE WAYS

To every man there openeth
  A choice of ways to go;
And the high soul takes the high road
  And the low soul takes the low,
And in between on misty flats,
  The rest drift to and fro;
But to everyone there openeth
  A high way and a low,
And everyone decideth
  The way his soul shall go.
           —*John Oxenham.*

What we truly and earnestly aspire to be, that in some sense we are. The mere aspiration, by changing the frame of mind, for the moment realizes itself.—*Mrs. Jameson.*

BUILDERS AND WRECKERS

"Look for the good things, not the faults. It takes a good deal bigger-sized brain to find out what is not wrong with people and things, than to find out what is wrong. The little man often actually rates his capacity by the number of things he can find the matter. The valuable fellow is the one who finds what isn't the matter and gives it a pat on the back."

A speck of dust may clog the works of a watch; mere stones derail the fastest express; miserable little ship-worms sink the proudest schooner; Marine vermin contrive to destroy the mightiest dikes.

But you would not dare to deduce therefrom that dust and boulders and crawfish are superior to clock-makers, mechanics, shipwrights and engineers.

An inventor may file away for decades at a revolutionary device, but the same rasp, in the grasp of a fool, can mangle his model in a dozen

Each is given a bag of tools,
A shapeless mass,
A book of rules;
And each must make,
Ere life is flown,
A stumbling-block
Or a stepping-stone.
                    —*R. L. Sharpe.*

THE BRIDGE BUILDER

An old man going a lone highway
Came at the evening, cold and gray,
To a chasm vast and deep and wide.
The old man crossed in the twilight dim,
The sudden stream had no fear for him;
But he turned when safe on the other side
And built a bridge to span the tide.
"Old man," said a fellow pilgrim near,
"You are wasting your strength with building
        here
Your journey will end with the ending day,
You never again will pass this way;
You've crossed the chasm deep and wide,
Why build you this bridge at eventide?"
The builder lifted his old gray head,
"Good friend, in the path I have come," he
        said,

"There followeth after me today
A youth, whose feet must pass this way;
This chasm, that has not been hard for me,
To that fair-haired youth may a pitfall be;
He too must cross in the twilight dim—
Good friend, I am building this bridge for him."
                                        —*Dromgoole.*

WHICH AM I?

I watched them tearing a building down,
A gang of men in a busy town,
With a ho-heave-ho and a lusty yell,
They swung a beam and a side wall fell.

I asked the foreman, "Are these men skilled?
And the men you'd hire if you had to build?"
He gave a laugh and said, "No indeed!
Just common labor is all I need."

"I can easily wreck in a day or two
What builders have taken a year to do."
And I thought to myself as I went my way,
Which of these roles have I tried to play?

Am I a builder who works with care,
Measuring life by the rule and square?
Am I shaping my deeds to a well-made plan,
Patiently doing the best I can?
Or am I a wrecker who walks the town,
Content with the labor of tearing down?

—*Anonymous.*

CHARACTER

True worth is in *being,* not *seeming*—
    In doing, each day that goes by,
Some little good—not in dreaming
    Of great things to do by and by.
For whatever men say in their blindness,
    And in spite of the fancies of youth,
There's nothing so kingly as kindness,
    And nothing so royal as truth.

—*Alice Cary.*

You will always have to live with yourself, and it is to your best interest to see that you have good company—a clean, pure, straight, honest, up-right, generous, magnanimous companion.

—*Orison Swett Marden.*

YOU

You are the fellow that has to decide
Whether you'll do it or toss it aside.
You are the fellow who makes up your mind
Whether you'll lead or linger behind;
Whether you'll try for the goal that's far,
Or just be contented to stay where you are.
Take it or leave it, here's something to do!
Just think it over—It's all up to you.
What do you wish? To be known as a shirk,
Or known as a good man who's willing to work?
Scorned as a loafer, or praised by your chief,
Rich man or poor man or beggar or thief?
Eager and earnest or dull through the day?
Honest or crooked? It's you must say.
You must decide in the face of the test
Whether you'll shirk or live it your best.

—*Edgar A. Guest.*

From Mr. Guest's book, *The Light of Faith,* Copyright
1926, used by permission of The Reilly & Lee Co.,
Chicago.

To think without confusion, clearly;
To love your fellowmen sincerely;
To act from honest motives purely;
To trust in God and Christ securely.
—*Henry Van Dyke.*

MYSELF

I have to live with myself, and so
I want to be fit for myself to know;
I want to be able as days go by
Always to look myself straight in the eye.
I don't want to stand, with the setting sun
And hate myself for the things I've done.
I want to go out with my head erect;
I want to deserve all men's respect;
While here in the struggle for fame and pelf
I want to be able to like myself.
I don't want to look at myself and know
That I'm bluster and bluff and empty show.
I never can fool myself; and so,
Whatever happens, I want to be
Self-respecting and conscience-free.

—Edgar A. Guest.

From *Collected Verse of Edgar A. Guest,* copyright 1934, used by permission of The Reilly & Lee Co., Chicago.

"Strength of character consists of two things—power of will and power of self restraint. It requires, therefore, for its existence, strong feelings and strong command over them."

It is not so much the greatness of our troubles, as the littleness of our spirit, which makes us complain.—*J. Taylor.*

MY CREED

To live as gently as I can,
  To be, no matter where a MAN.
To take what comes of good or ill
  And cling to faith and honor still.
To do my best and let that stand
  The record of my brain and hand.
And then should failure come to me,
  Still work and hope for victory.

To have no secret place wherein
  I stoop unseen to shame or sin.
To be the same when I'm alone
  As when my every deed is known.
To live undaunted and unafraid
  Of any step that I have made.
To be, without pretense or sham,
  Exactly what men think I am.

                    —*Edgar A. Guest.*

From *Collected Verse of Edgar A. Guest,* copyright 1934, used by permission of The Reilly & Lee Co., Chicago.

"Think not of yourself as merely the architect of your career; but as the sculptor. Expect to have to do a lot of hard hammering and chiselling and scraping and polishing."

I WOULD BE TRUE

———

I would be true, for there are those who trust me;
  I would be pure, for there are those who care;
I would be strong, for there is much to suffer;
  I would be brave, for there is much to dare.
I would be friend of all—the foe, the friendless;
  I would be giving and forget the gift.
I would be humble, for I know my weakness;
  I would look up—and laugh—and love—and lift.
                    —*Howard Arnold Walter.*

He who is false to present duty breaks a thread
in the loom, and will find the flaw when he may
have forgotten its cause.—*Beecher.*

True glory lies in noble deeds.—*Cicero.*

Let us have faith that right makes might and
in that faith let us, to the end, dare to do our
duty as we understand it.—*Abraham Lincoln.*

This above all—to thine own self be true;
And it must follow, as the night the day,
Thou canst not then be false to any man.
                    —*Shakespeare.*

A man without character is like a ship without a rudder.—*Dr. Maeser.*

SMILE WHEN IN TROUBLE

I love the man that can smile in trouble, that can gather strength from distress, and grow brave by reflection. It is the business of little minds to shrink, but he whose conscience approves his conduct, will pursue his principles unto death.
                                        —*Thomas Paine.*

"Rise to the stature of your better self."

I would rather be right than be president.
                                        —*Henry Clay.*

CHARITY

We should be lenient in our judgment, because often the mistakes of others would have been ours had we had the opportunity to make them.
                                        —*Dr. Alsaker.*

Though I speak with the tongues of men and of angels, and have not charity, I am become as sounding brass, or a tinkling cymbal.

And though I have the gift of prophecy, and understand all mysteries, and all knowledge; and though I have all faith so that I could remove mountains, and have not charity, I am nothing.

And though I bestow all my goods to feed the poor, and though I give my body to be burned, and have not charity, it profiteth me nothing.

Charity suffereth long, and is kind; charity envieth not; charity vaunteth not itself, is not puffed up,

Doth not behave itself unseemly, seeketh not her own, is not easily provoked, thinketh no evil;

Rejoiceth not in iniquity, but rejoiceth in the truth;

Beareth all things, believeth all things, hopeth all things, endureth all things.

Charity never faileth; but whether there be prophecies, they shall fail; whether there be tongues, they shall cease; whether there be knowledge, it shall vanish away.

For we know in part, and we prophesy in part.

But when that which is perfect is come, then that which is in part shall be done away.

When I was a child, I spake as a child, I understood as a child, I thought as a child; but when I became a man, I put away childish things.

For now we see through a glass, darkly; but then face to face; now I know in part; but then shall I know even as also I am known.

And now abideth faith, hope, charity, these three; but the greatest of these is charity.

—*I. Corinthians* 13.

Charity is the pure love of Christ, and it endureth forever; and whoso is found possessed of it at the last day it shall be well with him.

—*B. of M., Moroni* 7:47.

Charity should begin at home; but it should not stay there.—*Phillips Brooks.*

CHEERFULNESS

Cheerfulness is an excellent wearing quality. It has been called the bright weather of the heart. It gives harmony of soul and is a perpetual song without words. It is tantamount to respose. It enables nature to recruit its strength.—*Smiles.*

WHY DON'T YOU LAUGH?

Why don't you laugh, dear boys, when troubles
    come,
Instead of sitting 'round so sour and glum?
    You cannot have all play,
    And sunshine every day;
When troubles come, I say, why don't you laugh?

Why don't you laugh, dear girls? 'Twill ever
    help to soothe
    The aches and pains. No road in life is smooth;
    There's many an unseen bump,
    And many a hidden stump
O'er which you'll have to jump. Why don't you
laugh?

Why don't you laugh? Don't let your spirits wilt;
Don't sit and cry because the milk you've spilt;
    If you would mend it now,
    Pray let me tell you how:
Just milk another cow! Why don't you laugh?

Why don't you laugh, and make us all laugh, too,
And keep us mortals all from getting blue?
    A laugh will always win;
    If you can't laugh, just grin—
Come on, let's all join in! Why don't you laugh?
                                    —*Anonymous.*

SING AND SMILE AND PRAY

Sing the clouds away,
Night will turn to day—
If you sing and sing and sing
You'll sing the clouds away.

Smile the clouds away,
Night will turn to day—
If you smile and smile and smile
You'll smile the clouds away.

Pray the clouds away,
Pray and pray and pray—
Night will turn to day,
No matter what they say.

Sing and Smile and Pray,
That's the only way—
If you sing and smile and pray
You'll drive the clouds away.

                        —*The Brocks.*

"A smile is a light in the window of the soul
indicating that the heart is at home."

"If you keep your face turned toward the sun
all the shadows of life fall behind you."

SOLITUDE

Laugh, and the world laughs with you;
   Weep, and you weep alone.
For the sad old earth must borrow its mirth,
   But has trouble enough of its own.
Sing, and the hills will answer;
   Sigh, and its lost on the air.
The echos bound to a joyful sound,
   But shrink from voicing care.

—From *Poems of Passion,*
By *Ella Wheeler Wilcox,*

Used by permission of W. B. Conkley Co.

A cheerful man is one who can present a smiling face to every turn of fortune; not one whose radiance is skin-deep and disappears when shares are down or dinner is a trifle late.—*Leigh Smith.*

Cheerfulness of disposition is a great source of enjoyment in life, and it is also a great safeguard of character. It furnishes the best soil for the growth of goodness and virtue. It gives brightness to heart and elasticity of spirit. It is the companion of charity, the nurse of patience, the mother of wisdom. It is also the best of moral and mental tonics.—*Smiles.*

COMFORT

Let not your heart be troubled: ye believe in God, believe also in me.

In my Father's house are many mansions: if it were not so, I would have told you. I go to prepare a place for you.—*John* 14:1, 2.

Come unto me, all ye that labour and are heavy laden, and I will give you rest.

Take my yoke upon you, and learn of me; for I am meek and lowly in heart: and ye shall find rest unto your souls.

For my yoke is easy, and my burden is light.
—*Matt.* 11:28-30.

Of all created comforts, God is the lender; you are the borrower, not the owner.—*Rutherford.*

Sprinkled along the waste of years
Full many a soft green isle appears:
Pause where we may upon the desert road,
Some shelter is in sight, some sacred safe abode.
—*Keble.*

COMPANIONSHIP

———

COMPANIONSHIP

———

When folks say that I walk alone,
  With pity in their eyes,
I ever stand and stare at them
  In wondering surprise,
  Because they are too blind to see
    That in each breathing clod,
In sun and rain in grass and trees,
  I ever walk with God.
          —Edgar Daniel Kramer.

When we live habitually with the wicked, we become either their victim or their disciple; when we associate, with the virtuous men, we form ourselves in imitation of their virtues, or at least lose some of our faults.—*Agapet.*

In the society of thine equals thou shalt enjoy more pleasure; in the society of thy superiors thou shall find most profit.—*Quarles.*

A Persian fable says:
One day a wanderer found a lump of clay
   So redolent of sweet perfume
   Its odor scented all the room.
"What art thou?" was his quick demand
"Art thou some gem from Samarkand
   Or spikenard in this rude disguise,
   Or other costly merchandise?"
—"Nay: I am but a lump of clay."—Say!
   Then whence this wondrous perfume?"
—"Friend, if the secret I must disclose,
I have been dwelling with the rose."

                   —Anonymous.

COURAGE

They are slaves who fear to speak
For the fallen and the weak.
They are slaves who will not choose
Hatred, scoffing and abuse
Rather than in silence shrink
From the truths they needs must think.
They are slaves who dare not be
In the right with two or three.

             —James Russell Lowell.

THE TEST

The test of a man is the fight he makes
    The grit that he daily shows;
The way he stands on his feet and takes
    Fate's numerous bumps and blows.
A coward can smile when there's naught to fear,
    When nothing his progress bars
But it takes a man to stand up and cheer
    While some other fellow stars.

It isn't the victory after all
    But the fight that a brother makes.
The man, who, driven against the wall,
    Still stands up erect and takes
The blows of fate with his head held high
    Bleeding, and bruised and pale,
He's the man who'll win in the by and by,
    For he isn't afraid to fail.

It's the bumps you get and the jolts you get
    An the shocks that your courage stands,
The hours of sorrow and vain regret,
    The prize that escapes your hands,
That test your mettle and prove your worth.
    It isn't the blows you deal,
But the blows you take on this good old earth
    That shows if your stuff is real.

—Anonymous.

Courage isn't a brilliant dash,
A daring deed in a moment's flash;
It isn't an instantaneous thing
Born of despair with a sudden spring;
It isn't a creature of flickered hope
Or the final tug at a slipping rope;
But it's something deep in the soul of man
That is working always to serve some plan.

Courage isn't the last resort
In the work of life or the game of sport;
It isn't a thing that man can call
At some future time when he's apt to fall;
If he hasn't it now, he will have it not
When the strain is great and the pace is hot;
For who would strive for a distant goal
Must always have courage within his soul.

—*Edgar A. Guest.*

When things go wrong as they sometimes will,
And the road you're traveling seems all up-hill;
When funds are low and debts are high,
And you want to laugh but you have to sigh;
When cares are pressing you down a bit,
Rest if you must—but don't you quit.

—*Anonymous.*

KEEP ON FIGHTIN'

When things are breaking wrong for you
This is the thing you should do—
Grit your teeth, throw out your chest,
Wipe off your chin, pull down your vest;
Allow nothing to ban your way,
Fight harder still to win the day,
Then things are bound to come your way.

Don't claim that fortune passed your door
And gave your lucky neighbor more.
You'll find Old Lady Luck is for
The man who works and don't get sore—
No matter how the rain may pour.

If hard fate deals you out a slap,
Don't curl up like a yellow sap;
Bounce up and laugh at such a tap,
Knock all obstacles off the map
An show 'em how a man can rap.

When 'gainst the tide turn on more steam;
Any dead fish can float down stream.
To breast life's currents, take the tip;
It takes a live one, full of zip,
That nothing, short of death, can whip,
Just keep on fightin'.—*Anonymous.*

COURAGE

The man, who, when in peril, calmly stops and considers, and decides upon a certain mode of procedure, and then exerts his every energy to carry out his means, is the courageous man.

Courage is commonly applied in the sense of foolhardiness. But the courageous man is not he who sticks his head into the lion's mouth, and then pinches his tail, or the man who exposes himself to unnecessary danger in order to stand his ground. There may be more courage in a retreat than in a foolhardy, bold defense. He is courageous who has the courage to retreat when he knows the object of his combat would be bettered thereby.

Courage is also the ability to endure all kinds of hardships and exertions, in order to accomplish one's ends. The ability to survive defeats, disappointments and losses, also deserve mention as being closely related to and, indeed, part of courage.—*Preston D. Richards.*

Be strong and of good courage; be not afraid, neither be thou dismayed; for the Lord thy God is with thee whithersoever thou goest.

—*Joshua* 1:9.

I dare do all that may become a man, who dares do more is none.

—*Shakespeare.*

The courage we desire and prize is not the courage to die decently but to live manfully.

—*Carlyle.*

> Courage, brother! do not stumble,
>   Tho thy path be dark as night;
> There's a star to guide the humble—
>   "Trust in God and do the right."
> Let the road be dark and dreary,
>   And its end far out of sight,
> Face it bravely! strong or weary—
>   "Trust in God and do the right."
>   —*Norman Macleod.*

DEATH, IMMORTALITY, RESURRECTION

> Millions of years may pass away
> The sun no longer shines by day,
> The stars burn out and cease to be
> The earth freeze up from sea to sea,
> But time can never claim as toll
> The deathless substance of the soul.

Then how should you and how should I
Improve each hour that passes by
And mould and shape and perfect make
That soul which, though systems break
Lives on and through the eons be
Just what we make it, for eternity.

—Anon.

SUCH IS DYING

I am standing upon the seashore. A ship at my side spreads her white sails to the morning breeze and starts for the blue ocean. She is an object of beauty and strength and I stand and watch her until at length she hangs like a speck of white cloud just where the sea and sky come to mingle with each other. Then someone at my side says: "There! She's gone!"

Gone where? Gone from my sight, that is all. She is just as large in mast and hull and spar as she was when she left my side, and just as able to bear her load of living weight to the place of destination. Her diminished size is in me, not in her; and just at the moment when someone at my side says: "There! She's gone!" there are other eyes watching her coming and other voices ready to take up the glad shout, "Here she comes!"— and such is dying.—*Author Unknown.*

DEATH AND LIFE

We are so stupid about death. We will not learn
How it is wages paid to those who earn,
How it is gift for which on earth we yearn,
To be set free from bondage to the flesh;

How it is turning seed-corn into grain,
How it is winning Heaven's eternal gain,
How it means freedom evermore from pain,
How it untangles every mortal mesh.

We are so selfish about death. We count our
    grief
Far more than we consider their relief,
Whom the great Reaper gathers in the sheaf,
No more to know the season's constant change.

And we forget that it means only life,—
Life with all joy, peace, rest and glory rife,
The victory won, and ended all the strife,
And Heaven no longer far away and strange.

Their Lent is over and their Easter won.
Waiting till over Paradise the sun
Shall rise in majesty, and life begun
Shall glow in glory, as the perfect day
Moves on to hold its endless, deathless way.
                    —*Bishop William Croswell Doane.*

(*Said of the statue of the angel Moroni
atop the spire of the Salt Lake Temple.*)
It's just another piece of bronze
Uplifted to the coming dawns;
It's just another gilded form
Veiled in the sifting light of morn;
But that angel-crowned temple spire
Evokes the mystic's stirring lyre.
It is a heaven-sent token
That life's cycles are not broken;
For his trumpet call speaks to me
Of One back from the shoreless sea,
To re-kindle Faith's glowing flame
And give Easter its olden fame.
—*Nephi Jensen.*

So live that when thy summons comes to join
The innumerable caravan that moves
To that mysterious realm, where each shall take
His chamber in the silent halls of death,
Thou go not like the quarry slave at night,
Scourged to his dungeon, but sustained and
    soothed
By an unfaltering trust, approach thy grave
Like one who wraps the drapery of his couch
About him, and lies down to pleasant dreams.
—*William Cullen Bryant, in "Thanatopsis."*

THERE IS NO DEATH

There is no death! The stars go down
　　To rise upon some fairer shore;
And bright in Heaven's jewelled crown
　　They shine forevermore.

There is no death! The dust we tread
　　Shall change beneath the summer showers
To golden grain or mellowed fruit,
　　Or rainbow-tinted flowers.

There is no death! The leaves may fall
　　And flowers may fade and pass away;
They only wait through wintry hours
　　The coming of the May.

There is no death! An angel form
　　Walks o'er the earth with silent tread;
He bears our best loved things away,
　　And then we call them dead.
　　　　　　　　　　　　—Bulwer Lytton.

Why should it be thought a thing incredible that
God should raise the dead?—*Paul to Agrippa.*

The spirit and the body are the soul of man.
And the resurrection from the dead is the re-
demption of the soul.—*D. & C.* 88:15, 16.

FRANKLIN'S SELF-WRITTEN EPITAPH

The Body
of
Benjamin Franklin, Printer
(Like the cover of an old book,
Its contents torn out,
And stripped of its lettering and gilding,)
Lies here, food for worms.
Yet the work itself shall not be lost,
For it will (as he believes) appear once
more
In a new
And more beautiful Edition
Corrected and Amended
By
The Author

Our birth is but a sleep and a forgetting;
The soul that rises with us, our life's star
Hath had elsewhere its setting,
And cometh from afar;
Not in entire forgetfulness,
And not in utter nakedness,
But trailing clouds of glory do we come
From God who is our home.—*Wordsworth,*
in *"Ode on Intimations of Immortality."*

Verily, verily, I say unto you, The hour is coming, and now is, when the dead shall hear the voice of the Son of God; and they that hear shall live.

For as the Father hath life in himself; so hath he given to the Son to have life in himself;

And hath given him authority to execute judgment also, because he is the Son of man.

Marvel not at this: for the hour is coming, in the which all that are in the graves shall hear his voice,

And shall come forth; they that have done good, unto the resurrection of life: and they that have done evil, unto the resurrection of damnation.—*John* 5:25-29.

I am the resurrection, and the life; he that believeth in me, though he were dead, yet shall he live; and whosoever liveth and believeth on me shall never die.—*John* 11:25, 26.

Life is real! Life is earnest!
　And the grave is not its goal;
Dust thou art, to dust returnest,
　Was not spoken of the soul.
　　—*From Longfellow's "Psalm of Life."*

IF EASTER BE NOT TRUE

If Easter be not true,
Then faith must mount on broken wing;
Then love no more immortal spring;
Then hope must lose her mighty urge;
Life prove a phantom, death a dirge—
    If Easter be not true.

If Easter be not true—
But it IS true, and Christ is risen!
And mortal spirit from its prison
Of sin and death with him may rise!
Worth-while the struggle, sure the prize,
    Since Easter, aye, is true!
                        —*Barstow.*

There are also celestial bodies, and bodies terrestrial: but the glory of the celestial is one, and the glory of the terrestrial is another.

There is one glory of the sun, and another glory of the moon, and another glory of the stars: for one star differeth from another star in glory.

So also is the resurrection of the dead.

                        —1 *Cor.* 15:40-42.

"To live is to go on a journey;
To die is to come back home."

Press onward through each varying hour;
Let no weak fears thy course delay;
Immortal being! feel thy power,
Pursue thy bright and endless way.
—*Andrews Norton.*

Be of good cheer about death, and know this of a truth, that no evil can happen to a good man, either in life or after death.—*Socrates.*

This is my work and my glory, to bring to pass the immortality and eternal life of man.
—*P. of G. P., Moses* 1:39.

DEBT

Some people who buy on time don't know when time leaves off and eternity begins.—*Fay Egan.*

Debt is the fatal disease of republics; the first thing and the mightiest to undermine government and corrupt people.—*Wendell Phillips.*

Never be argued out of your soul; never be argued out of your honor, and never be argued into believing that soul and honor do not run a terrible risk if you limp into life with the load of debt on your shoulders.—*Bulwer Lytton.*

DEITY

O MY FATHER

O my Father, thou that dwellest
　In the high and glorious place!
When shall I regain thy presence
　And again behold thy face?
In thy holy habitation,
　Did my spirit once reside;
In my first primeval childhood,
　Was I nurtured near thy side.

For a wise and glorious purpose
　Thou hast placed me here on earth,
And withheld the recollection
　Of my former friends and birth.
Yet ofttimes a secret something
　Whispered, "You're a stranger here,"
And I felt that I had wandered
　From a more exalted sphere.

I had learned to call thee Father,
　Through thy Spirit from on high;
But until the Key of Knowledge
　Was restored, I knew not why.

In the heavens are parents single?
  No; the thought makes reason stare!
Truth is reason, truth eternal
  Tells me I've a mother there.

When I leave this frail existence,
  When I lay this mortal by,
Father, Mother, may I meet you
  In your royal courts on high?
Then, at length, when I've completed
  All you sent me forth to do,
With your mutual approbation,
  Let me come and dwell with you.
                    —*Eliza R. Snow.*

Men must be governed by God or they will be
ruled by tyrants.—*William Penn.*

MYSTERY

I stood in a lovely garden one night—
And I marveled at the enchanting sight!
When lo! There, in the Cathedral-like hush
I heard the swish of a painter's brush.
I saw the flowers and the trees in prayer,
And knew the Great Gardener was working there!
                    —*Frances Angermayer.*

How often down the path of life
In darkness man has trod;
When if he had but raised his head
He would have seen his God!
—*Waldo G. Cook.*

GOD, AN EXALTED MAN

God himself was once as we are now, and is an exalted man, and sits enthroned in yonder heavens! That is the great secret. If the veil were rent today, and the great God who holds this world in its orbit, and who upholds all worlds and all things by his power, was to make himself visible, I say, if you were to see him today, you would see him like a man in form—like yourselves in all the person, image, and very form as a man; for Adam was created in the very fashion, image and likeness of God, and received instruction from, and walked, talked and conversed with him, as one man talks and communes with another.—Joseph Smith (T.P.J.S. p. 345.)

The Father has a body of flesh and bones as tangible as man's; the Son also; but the Holy Ghost has not a body of flesh and bones, but is a personage of Spirit.—*D. & C.* 130:22.

TO NATIONS THAT BURY GOD

Your lights go out one by one.
Even the brightness of the sun.
You held a funeral for God.
You buried Him deep in the sod.
He is gone. You won the fight.
Why then do you tremble tonight?
God sleeps in His coffin, O men.
You claim He cannot come again.
What do you fear?   God is not there.
Why such horror in your vacant stare?
Ashen-faced, you shriek in the gloom.
Fools!—You buried yourselves in His tomb.

—*Frances Angermayer.*

And this is life eternal, that they might know thee the only true God, and Jesus Christ, whom thou hast sent.—*John* 17:3.

DISCOURAGEMENT

BEWARE OF THE EVIL TOOL

A Chinese legend describes how the father of Sin decided to have a sale and dispose of all his tools to anyone who would pay his price.

The implements were laid out in a row for inspection and among others were tools labeled "Malice," "Envy," "Hatred," "Jealousy" and "Deceit." Every one had a price tag on it. Apart from the others lay a harmless-looking, wedge-shaped tool, very much worn from use, that was priced a great deal higher than the rest.

One of the buyers asked the Devil what it was. "That," he answered, "is Discouragement; and it's in fine shape."

"But why have you priced it so high?"

"Because it is more useful to me than any of the others. I can pry open and get inside a man's consciousness with that wedge when I couldn't get near him with any of the others. And believe me, once I do get inside I can use that man in whatever way suits me best. Of course, you'll notice it is well worn. That's because I use it with nearly everybody, for very few of you mortals know that it belongs to me."

However, the price was so high that this particular tool was never sold. The Devil still owns it, and is still using it.—*The Ambassador.*

"Discouragement is like a baby, the more you nurse it, the bigger it grows."

DUTY

It is our privilege to be so fastened to our line of duty that we cannot be turned away by the strongest current of temptation.—*Dr. Maeser.*

Let us all do the will of our Father in heaven today, and we will then be prepared for the duty of tomorrow, and for the eternities to come.

—*Pres. Heber J. Grant*

He who is false to present duty breaks a thread in the loom, and will find the flaw when he may have forgotten its cause.

—*Henry Ward Beecher.*

The consideration that human happiness and moral duty are inseparably connected will always continue to prompt me to promote the progress of the former by inculcating the practice of the latter.

—*Washington.*

ENTHUSIASM

"You cannot kindle a fire in any other heart until it is burning in your own."

Nothing great was ever achieved without enthusiasm.—*Emerson.*

> I gaze upon the thousand stars
>   That fill the midnight sky;
> And wish, so passionately wish,
>   A light like theirs on high.
> I have such eagerness of hope
>   To benefit my kind;
> I feel as if immortal power
>   Were given to my mind.
> —*Miss Landon.*

I would rather have the ardor of my soldiers and they half trained, than have the best fighting machine in Europe without this element.
—*Napoleon.*

EXAMPLE

THE LOST SHEEP

'Twas a sheep, not a lamb, that strayed away,
In the parable Jesus told;
A grown-up sheep that had gone astray,
From the ninety and nine in the fold.

Out on the hillside, out in the cold,
'Twas a sheep the good shepherd sought,
And back to the flock safe into the fold
'Twas a sheep the good shepherd brought.

And why for the sheep should we earnestly long,
And as earnestly hope and pray,
Because there is danger, if they go wrong,
They will lead the lambs astray.
For the lambs will follow the sheep, you know,
Wherever the sheep may stray;
When the sheep go wrong, it will not be long
Till the lambs are as wrong as they.

And so with the sheep we earnestly plead,
For the sake of the lambs today;
If the lambs are lost; what a terrible cost
Some sheep will have to pay.—*C. D. Miller.*

EXAMPLE   55

Ye are the light of the world. A city that is set on an hill cannot be hid.

Neither do men light a candle, and put in under a bushel, but on a candlestick; and it giveth light unto all that are in the house.

Let your light so shine before men, that they may see your good works, and glorify your Father which is in heaven.—*Matt.* 5:14-16.

Children have more need of models than of critics.—*Joubert.*

Whatever parent gives his children good instruction, and sets them at the same time a bad example, brings them food in one hand and poison in the other.—*Balguy.*

If thou desirest to see thy child virtuous, let him not see his father's vices: thou canst not rebuke that in children that they behold practiced in thee; till reason be ripe, examples direct more than precepts; as thy behavior is before thy children's faces, such commonly is theirs behind their parents' backs.

—*Quarles.*

FAITH

WHAT IS FAITH?

We live by faith—what is faith? but to say
"I take Thy hand, O Lord, lead Thou the way;
For without Thee as Guide I dare not go;
Gladly I take the pathway Thou dost show;
Teach me Thy will to do;
I trust Thee, for I know that Thou art true."

To feel whatever comes, though dark the way,
Secure in Thee; more confident each day
That Thou are good.—Thy hand is guiding me;
I fear no ill nor ask my way to see;
Serene my soul can rest;
For all that Thou dost plan for me is best.

—Emily Hersey.

"No man is to be pitied except the one whose future lies behind him, in other words—the man who has lost faith in himself and is sinking because he refuses to swim."

Youth without faith is a day without sun.

—Onida.

Is any sick among you? let him call for the elders
of the church; and let them pray over him, anoint-
ing him with oil in the name of the Lord;

And the prayer of faith shall save the sick, and
the Lord shall raise him up; and if he have committed sins, they shall be forgiven him.

—James 5:14, 15.

Colonel Lawrence of Arabian fame tells how
an Arab shiek, after hearing the Western scholar
recount the wonders revealed by the telescope,
said: "You foreigners see millions of stars, and
nothing beyond. We Arabs see only a few stars—
and God."—*"They Tell a Story."*

Faith without works is like a bird without wings;
though she may hop with her companions on
earth, yet she will never fly with them to heaven.

—J. Beaumont.

God never would send the darkness
  If He felt we could bear the light.
But we would not cling to His guiding hand
  If the way were always bright;
And we would not care to walk by faith
  Could we always walk by sight.—*Anonymous.*

GOD'S BANK AIN'T BUSTED YET

The bank had closed; my earthly store
    had vanished from my hand,
I felt there was no sadder one than I
    in all the land.
My washerwoman, too, had lost her little
    mite with mine,
Yet she was singing as she hung the
    washing on the line.
"How can you be so gay," I asked,
    "your loss, don't you regret?"
"Yes, ma'am, but what's the use to fret?
    God's Bank ain't busted yet."

I felt my burden lighter grow,
    her faith I seemed to share;
In prayer I went to God's great throne
    and laid my trouble there.
The sun burst from behind the clouds,
    in golden splendor set;
I thank the Giver of it all,
    "God's Bank ain't busted yet.'

And now I draw rich dividends,
    more than my hand can hold;
Of faith and love and hope and trust:
    and peace of mind untold.

I thanked the Giver of it all,
    but still I can't forget,
My washerwoman's simple words,
    "God's Bank ain't busted yet."

O weary one upon life's road,
    when everything seems drear,
And losses loom on every hand,
    and skies seem not too clear;
Throw back your shoulders, lift your head
    and cease to chafe and fret,
Your dividends will be declared—
    "God's Bank ain't busted yet."
                 —*Anonymous.*

Trust in the Lord with all thine heart; and lean not unto thine own understanding. In all thy ways acknowledge him, and he will direct thy paths.— *Proverbs* 3:5, 6.

"A great many Christians would probably give God a handful of meal after He had filled the barrel; but they would hesitate to give Him the last handful on His promise to fill the barrel when empty."

"I would rather walk in the dark with Thee,
  Than walk alone in the light.
I would rather walk by faith with Thee.
  Than walk alone by sight."

Jesus saith unto him, Thomas, because thou
hast seen me, thou hast believed: blessed are they
that have not seen, and yet have believed.

—John 20:29.

FAITH

———

In my doubts' darkest night
  My thoughts are still serene;
By soul's inerrant sight
  I can see the unseen.

My creed needs no defense,
  My quiet soul has not erred;
By inner, faultless sense
  I can hear the unheard.

My heart is outstretching,
  Seraphic heights I own;
By soul's sure upreaching,
  I know the deep unknown.

—Nephi Jensen.

All the strength and force of man comes from his faith in things unseen. He who believes is strong; he who doubts is weak. Strong convictions precede great actions. The man strongly possessed of an idea is the master of all who are uncertain or wavering. Clear, deep living convictions rule the world.—*James Freeman Clarke*.

FAITH INSURANCE

Live a clean life.
Pray earnestly and often.
    Study to know the truth.
    Honor the Priesthood.
        Attend Sacrament meeting regularly.
        Keep the Word of Wisdom.
            Pay an honest tithing.

                        —*E. L. M.*

If faith produce no works, I see
That faith is not a living tree.
Thus faith and works together grow;
No separate life they e'er can know;
They're soul and body, hand and heart;
What God hath joined, let no man part.
                        —*Hannah More*.

FAULT-FINDING

———

Nothing is easier than fault-finding; no talent, no self-denial, no brains, no character are required to set up in the grumbling business.—*Robert West.*

How good it would be if we could learn to be rigorous in judgment of ourselves, and gentle in our judgment of our neighbors! In remedying defects, kindness works best with others, sternness with ourselves. It is easy to make allowances for our faults, but dangerous; hard to make allowances for others' faults, but wise. "If thy hand offend thee, cut if off," is a word for our sins; for the sins of others, "Father, forgive them."
—*Maltbie Babcock.*

REPROVING ADVICE

———

"It was my custom in my youth," says a celebrated Persian writer, "to rise from my sleep, to watch, pray, and read the Koran. One night, as I was thus engaged my father, a man of practiced virtue, awoke. 'Behold,' said I to him, 'thy chil-

dren are lost in irreligious slumbers, while I alone
wake to praise God.' 'Son of my soul,' said he,
'it is better to sleep than to wake to remark the
faults of thy brethren.' "

—*"They Tell a Story."*

FEAR

An Arab folk tale relates that Pestilence once
met a caravan upon the desert-way to Bagdad.
"Why," asked the Arab chief, "must you hasten to
Bagdad?"

"To take 5,000 lives," Pestilence replied.

Upon the way back from the City of the Caliphs,
Pestilence and the caravan met again. "You
deceived me," the chief said angrily. "Instead of
5,000 lives, you took 50,000!"

"Nay," said Pestilence. "Five thousand and
not one more. It was Fear who killed the rest."

—*Maurice Duhamel, "They Tell a Story."*

We may boldly say, the Lord is my helper, and
I will not fear what man shall do unto me.

—*Hebrews* 13:6.

Fear is always more painful to cowardice than death to true courage.—*Sir Philip Sidney.*

FORGIVENESS

His heart was as great as the world, but there was no room in it to hold the memory of a wrong.
—*Emerson.*

Never does the human soul appear so strong and noble as when it foregoes revenge, and forgives an injury.—*Chapin.*

Little vicious minds abound with anger and revenge, and are incapable of feeling the pleasure of forgiving their enemies.—*Chesterfield.*

Then came Peter to him, and said, Lord, how oft shall my brother sin against me, and I forgive him? till seven times?

Jesus saith unto him, I say not unto thee, until seven times; but until seventy times seven.
—*Matthew* 18:21, 22.

Wherefore, I say unto you, that ye ought to forgive one another; for he that forgiveth not his brother his trespasses standeth condemned before the Lord; for there remaineth in him the greater sin.

I, the Lord, will forgive whom I will forgive, but of you it is required to forgive all men.

—*D. & C.* 64:9, 10.

The narrow soul knows not the God-like glory of forgiving.—*Rowe.*

He who has not forgiven an enemy has never yet tasted one of the most sublime enjoyments of life.—*Lavater.*

And be ye kind one to another, tender-hearted, forgiving one another, even as God for Christ's sake hath forgiven you.—*Paul* (*Eph.* 4:32.)

For if ye forgive men their trespasses, your heavenly Father will also forgive you.

But if ye forgive not men their trespasses, neither will your Father forgive your trespasses.

—*Matthew* 6:14, 15.

He that cannot forgive others, breaks the bridge over which he must pass himself, for every man hath need to be forgiven.—*E. Herbert.*

FREEDOM AND FREE AGENCY

Wherefore, the Lord God gave unto man that he should act for himself. Wherefore, man could not act for himself save it should be that he was enticed by the one or the other.—*2 Nephi* 2:16.

> Know this, that every soul is free
> To choose his life and what he'll be,
> For this eternal truth is given,
> That God will force no man to heaven.
>
> He'll call, persuade, direct aright—
> Bless with wisdom, love and light—
> In nameless ways be good and kind,
> But never force the human mind.
> —*William C. Clegg.*

There are two freedoms—the false, where a man is free to do what he likes; the true, where he is free to do what he ought.—*Charles Kingsley.*

God who gave us life gave us liberty. Can the liberties of a nation be secure when we have removed a conviction that these liberties are the gift of God? Indeed I tremble for my country when I reflect that God is just, that his justice cannot sleep forever.—*Thomas Jefferson.*

One fact stands out in bold relief in the history of man's attempts for betterment. When compulsion is used only resentment is aroused, and the end is not gained. Only through moral suasion and appeal to men's reason can a movement succeed.—*Samuel Gompers.*

FRIENDS AND FRIENDSHIP

A little more kindness, A little less creed,
A little more giving, A little less greed,
A little more smile, A little less frown,
A little less kicking, A man when he's down,
A little more "we," A little less "I,"
A little more laugh, A little less cry,
A little more flowers, On the pathway of life,
And fewer on graves, At the end of the strife.

—*Anon.*

I HAVE A FRIEND!

I have a friend! A friend who is true!
A friend I can tell every sorrow to.
I have a friend who stands by my side.
A friend to whom all things I confide.
I have a friend—one beyond compare!
Oh, World, a loyal friend is rare.
I have a friend who passed the test.
I have a friend! — I am truly blessed!
                    —*Frances Angermayer.*

Friendship a peculiar boon of heaven,
  The noble mind's delight and pride,
To men and angels only given,
  To all the lower world denied.
                    —*Samuel Johnson.*

  "Words are easy like the wind;
  Faithful friends are hard to find."

  "If thou hast a thousand friends
  Thou hast none to spare;
  If thou hast a single enemy,
  Thou wilt meet him everywhere."

A foe to God was ne'er a true friend to man;
Some sinister intent taints all he does.
—Young.

If I knew you and you knew me,
If both of us could clearly see,
And with an inner sight divine
The meaning of your heart and mine,
I'm sure that we would differ less
And clasp our hands in friendliness.
Our thoughts would pleasantly agree
If I knew you and you knew me.
—Waterman.

"Friend is a word of royal tone,
Friend is a poem all alone."

A man that hath friends must show himself
friendly.—*Proverbs* 18:24.

But oh, if grief thy steps attend,
If want, if sickness be thy lot,
And thou require a soothing friend,
Forget me not! forget me not!
—Mrs. Opie.

GIVING

Not what we give, but what we share,
For the gift without the giver is bare;
Who gives himself with his alms feeds three—
Himself, his hungry neighbor and Me.
                                    —*James Russell Lowell.*

All who joy would win
Must share it, happiness was born a twin.
                                    —*Byron.*

Every man goes down to his death bearing in
his hands only that which he has given away.
                                    —*Persian Proverb.*

The best thing to give to your enemy is for-
giveness; to an opponent, tolerance; to a friend,
your heart; to your child, a good example; to a
father, deference; to your mother, conduct that
will make her proud of you; to yourself, respect;
to all men, charity.—*Mrs. Balfour.*

LIFE'S MIRROR

There are loyal hearts, there are spirits brave,
There are souls that are pure and true,
Then give to the world the best you have,
And the best will come back to you.

Give love, and love to your life will flow,
A strength in your utmost need,
Have faith, and a score of hearts will show
Their faith in your word and deed.

Give truth, and your gift will be paid in kind;
And honor will honor meet;
And a smile that is sweet will surely find
A smile that is just as sweet.

For life is the mirror of king and slave.
'Tis just what we are and do;
Then give to the world the best you have,
And the best will come back to you.

—*Madeline Bridges.*

In giving, a man receives more than he gives;
and the more is in proportion to the worth of the
thing given.—*George McDonald.*

GOSSIP

———

Believe not each accusing tongue,
  As most weak persons do;
But still believe that story wrong,
  Which ought not to be true.
                    —*Sheridan.*

"All the water in the seven seas cannot sink a ship if none gets inside."

"Before the word is spoken you must govern it. After it is spoken it will govern you."

THINK BEFORE YOU SPEAK

———

Suppose a neighbor has gone wrong?
  Think before you speak!
Each life must have some saddened song,
  Think before you speak!
You may have a grief some day
That will lead your feet astray;
Then you'll bless the tongues that say
  "Think before you speak!"

A neighbor's boy has "got in bad"—
    Think before you speak!
Recall his loved ones, shamed and sad,
    Think before you speak!
Some day your own son may fall;
Scorn may push him to the wall;
Then your heart will fill with gall—
    Think before you speak!

If some poor girl has slipped in woe,
    Think before you speak!
Say no harsh word to weight the blow.
    Think before you speak!
Scarlet letters yet may be
Hung upon your family tree;
Let us all have charity—
    Think before you speak!
                    —*David V. Bush.*

    Boys flying kites
        Haul in their white winged birds;
    You can't do that
        When you're flying words.
    Thoughts unexpressed
        May fall back dead;
    But even God can't kill them
        Once they're said.—*Anon.*

NAY, SPEAK NO ILL

Nay, speak no ill, a kindly word
  Can never leave a sting behind;
And oh, to breathe each tale we've heard,
  Is far beneath a noble mind.
Full oft a better seed is sown
  By choosing thus the kinder plan,
For, if but little good is known,
  Still let us speak the best we can.

Give me the heart that fain would hide—
  Would fain another's faults efface:
How can it please the human pride
  To prove humanity but base?
No, let us reach a higher mood—
  A nobler estimate of man,
Be earnest in the search for good,
  And speak of all the best we can.

Then speak no ill, but lenient be
  To others' failings as your own;
If you're the first a fault to see,
  Be not the first to make it known.
For life is but a passing day,
  No lip may tell how brief its span;
Then, O the little time we stay,
  Let's speak of all the best we can.

—Selected.

GRATITUDE

FATHER IN HEAVEN, WE THANK THEE

For the newness and the brightness of the spring-
time;
For the peacefulness of summer, over all;
For the whiteness and the cleanness of the winter;
For the mass of gorgeous colors in the fall—
Father in Heaven, we thank Thee.
For the sweetness and the laughter of small chil-
dren;
For the binding ties of brotherhood, sincere;
For the solace and the comfort Thou canst give us,
When we kneel in prayer and feel that Thou art
near—
Father in Heaven, we thank Thee.

For our noble spirit-birth in pre-existence;
For the lessons Thou art teaching mortal man;
For the satisfying hope of life-eternal;
For the knowledge we have gained of Thy great
plan—
Father in Heaven, we thank Thee.

—*Lizzie O. Borgeson White.*

HEAVEN AND HELL

Therefore, it (the earth) must needs be sanctified from all unrighteousness, that it may be prepared for the celestial glory;

For after it hath filled the measure of its creation, it shall be crowned with glory, even with the presence of God the Father;

That bodies who are of the celestial kingdom may possess it forever and ever; for, for this intent was it made and created, and for this intent are they sanctified.

And they who are not sanctified through the law which I have given unto you, even the law of Christ, must inherit another kingdom, even that of a terrestrial kingdom, or that of a telestial kingdom.

For he who is not able to abide the law of a celestial kingdom cannot abide a celestial glory.

And he who cannot abide the law of a terrestrial kingdom cannot abide a terrestrial glory.

And he who cannot abide the law of a telestial kingdom cannot abide a telestial glory; therefore he is not meet for a kingdom of glory. Therefore he must abide a kingdom which is not a kingdom of glory.   —D. & C. 88:18-24.

"Hell is the knowledge of opportunity lost — the place where the man I am comes face to face with the man I might have been."

Heaven is not gained at a single bound;
But we must build the ladder by which we rise
From lowly earth to vaulted skies,
And we mount to its summit, round by round.
                              —*J. G. Holland.*

Heaven's gates are not so highly arched as princes' palaces; they that enter there must go upon their knees.—*Daniel Webster.*

If our Creator has so bountifully provided for our existence here, which is but momentary, and for our temporal wants, which will soon be forgotten, how much more must he have done for our enjoyment in the everlasting world!
                              —*Hosea Ballou.*

The heavens is a place where God dwells and all his holy angels . . . and he looketh down upon all the children of men; and he knoweth all the thoughts and intents of their hearts.
                              —*B. of M. Alma* 18:30-32.

HONESTY

I hope I shall always possess firmness and virtue enough to maintain what I consider the most enviable of all titles, the character of an "Honest Man."—*Washington.*

Honesty is the best policy.—*Cervantes.*

My word shall always be as good as my bond.
—*Dr. Karl G. Maeser.*

Everything that thou reprovest in another, thou must most carefully avoid in thyself.—*Cicero.*

He that departs with his own honesty
For vulgar praise, doth it too dearly buy.
—*Ben Jonson.*

He that cheats another is a knave; but he that cheats himself is a fool.—*Dr. Maeser.*

There is no terror, Cassius, in your threats,
For I am armed so strong in honesty
That they pass me by as the idle wind.
Which I respect not.

—*Julius Caesar.*

INDUSTRY

For behold, it is not meet that I should command in all things; for he that is compelled in all things, the same is a slothful and not a wise servant; wherefore he receiveth no reward.

Verily I say, men should be anxiously engaged in a good cause, and do many things of their own free will, and bring to pass much righteousness;

For the power is in them, wherein they are agents unto themselves. And inasmuch as men do good they shall in nowise lose their reward.

—*D. & C.* 58:26-28.

Dost thou love life: Then do not squander time, for that is the stuff life is made of.

—*Benjamin Franklin.*

"When you stop rowing, you start down stream."

"Improve time, and time will improve you."

Sloth makes all things difficult; but Industry, all easy; and he that rises late must trot all day, and shall scarce overtake his business at night; while Laziness travels so slowly that Poverty soon overtakes him.—*Franklin*.

INITIATIVE

INITIATIVE

The world bestows its big prizes, both in money and honors for but one thing; and that is Initiative. What is Initiative? I'll tell you; It is doing the right thing without being told. But next to doing the thing without being told is to do it when you are told once. That is to say, carry the Message to Garcia: those who can carry a message get high honors but, their pay is not always in proportion. Next there are those who do the right thing only when necessity kicks them from behind, and these get indifference instead of honors, and a pittance for pay. This kind spends most of its time polishing a bench with a hard-luck story. Then, still lower down the scale than this, we have the fellow who will not do the right thing even when some one goes along to show him how and stays to see that he does it. He is always out of a job, and receives, the contempt that he deserves, unless he happens to have a rich Pa, in which case Destiny patiently awaits around the corner with a stuffed club.

To which class do you belong?

—*Elbert Hubbard.*

It is better to err on the side of initiative than inactivity.—*B. C. Forbes.*

FOLKS ARE LIKE BOATS

Some folks are like row-boats, for they have to be pulled wherever they go. Sometimes it is a hard struggle to keep them pointed in the right direction.

Others are like sail-boats. If the wind blows east, that's their direction. If it blows west, they go that way. Of course, it is possible for them to "beat against the wind," but they don't often do it. They are inclined to follow every wind of emotion and popular sentiment.

Others still are like power-boats who drive against the wind or tide and, in the face of great difficulties, keep their even course.

Which will you try to be like?

—Saturday Morning Review.

Do the thing and you shall have the power.

—Emerson.

JUDGING

Ye shall know them by their fruits. Do men gather grapes of thorns, or figs of thistles?

Even so every good tree bringeth forth good fruit; but a corrupt tree bringeth forth evil fruit.

A good tree cannot bring forth evil fruit, neither can a corrupt tree bring forth good fruit.

Every tree that bringeth not forth good fruit is hewn down, and cast into the fire.

Wherefore by their fruits ye shall know them.

—Matthew 7:16-20.

TRUTH REFLECTS UPON OUR SENSES

Once I said unto another,
　　In thine eye there is a mote;
If thou are a friend, a brother,
　　Hold, and let me pull it out.
But I could not see it fairly,
　　For my sight was very dim;
When I came to search more clearly,
　　In mine eye there was a beam.

If I love my brother dearer,
　　And his mote I would erase,
Then the light should shine the clearer,
　　For the eye's a tender place.
Others I have oft reproved,
　　For an object like a mote;
Now I wish this beam removed,
　　Oh, that tears would wash it out!

Charity and love are healing,
　　These will give the clearest sight;
When I saw my brother's failing,
　　I was not exactly right.
Now I'll take no further trouble,
　　Jesus' love is all my theme;
Little motes are but a bubble,
　　When I think upon the beam.
　　　　　　　　—*Eliza R. Snow.*

Judge not, that ye be not judged.

For with what judgment ye judge, ye shall be judged: and with what measure ye mete, it shall be measured to you again.

And why beholdest thou the mote that is in thy brother's eye, but considerest not the beam that is in thine own eye?

Or how wilt thou say to thy brother, Let me pull out the mote out of thine eye; and, behold, a beam is in thine own eye?

Thou hypocrite, first cast out the beam out of thine own eye; and then shalt thou see clearly to cast out the mote out of thy brother's eye.

—*Matthew* 7:1-5.

A traveler visited a church in Germany famous for its stained-glass windows. The exterior was plain, there was no beauty in the windows from the outside—there never is.

The first look within was a disappointment. The guide bade him go forward and look eastward where the sun was rising. Lo, a marvelous vision broke upon him of Jesus in the temple with the doctors. It was called 'The Glory of Christ.' He was filled with ecstasy.

The guide asked him to return about noon. Another window flamed in the sun with Christ walking upon the sea. He was requested to come yet again at sunset, and the rays fell upon Christ on the cross, amazingly touching and convincing.

Many people see nothing to admire in the Christian church. It is a disappointment, a fraud, a delusion. There are always people who see it from without. There are some inside who view it from the wrong angle, or on a dark and foggy day; they see only the pews and the floor. Those who come inside and look toward the sun see the glory of Christ, his power, and his salvation.

—*Onward.*

Let each man learn to know himself;
　　To gain that knowledge let him labor
To improve those failings in himself
　　Which he condemns so in his neighbor.
How leniently our own faults we view,
　　And conscience's voice adeptly smother;
Yet, oh, how harshly we review
　　The selfsame failings in another!

And if you meet an erring one
　　Whose deeds are blamable and thoughtless,
Consider, ere you cast the stone,
　　If you yourself be pure and faultless.

Oh, list to that small voice within,
  Whose whisperings oft make men confounded,
And trumpet not another's sin.
  You'd blush deep if your own were sounded.

And in self-judgment if you find
  Your deeds to others are superior,
To you has Providence been kind,
  As you should be to those inferior.
Example sheds a genial ray
  Of light, which men are apt to borrow,
So first improve yourself today,
  And then improve your friends tomorrow.
                              —*Anonymous.*

We should be lenient in our judgment because
often the mistakes of others would have been ours
had we had the opportunity to make them.
                              —*Dr. Alsaker.*

KINDNESS

"Don't expect to enjoy the cream of life if you
keep your milk of human kindness all bottled up."

KIND WORDS ARE SWEET TONES

Let us oft speak kind words to each other,
    At home or where'er we may be;
Like the warblings of birds on the heather,
    The tones will be welcome and free;
They'll gladden the heart that's repining,
    Give courage and hope from above;
And where the dark clouds hide the shining,
    Let in the bright sun-light of love.

Oh, the kind words we give shall in memory
        live,
    And sunshine forever impart;
Let us oft speak kind words to each other,
    Kind words are sweet tones of the heart.
                        —J. L. Townshend.

Since trifles make the sum of human things,
And half our misery from our foibles springs;
Since life's best joys consist in peace and ease,
And few can save or serve, but all may please;
Oh! let the ungentle spirit learn from hence
A small unkindness is a great offense,
Large bounties to bestow we wish in vain,
But all may shun the guilt of giving pain.
                        —Hannah More.

THANKS

Thanks for the smile you gave me today.—
You'll never know how it paved my way
With joy.—How it made everything right.—
Thanks.—Now,—I'm not afraid of the night.
Thanks for the kind word.—I didn't tell you,
But I held it close the long day through.—
Your kind words made me brave in a trial.
Thanks for your kindness.—Thanks for your
    smile.—   —*Frances Angermayer.*

KINDLINESS

Just a little act of kindness,
Just a little word of cheer,
Help to make our living pleasant,
Minimize both doubt and fear.

Jesus said, "Be meek and lowly,"
And He governs men with love,
Just as God, our Heavenly Father,
Governs in that Court above.

Jesus never hurt the feelings
Of a person, great or small;
Always He was kind and friendly—
We're assured He loves us all.

All the world is now in turmoil
Caused by gross unfriendliness.
Peace will follow Christian living—
Be the watchword Kindliness.
—*Lizzie O. Borgeson White.*

LEARNING AND WISDOM

"If wisdom's way you wisely seek
Five things observe with care—
Of whom you speak, to whom you speak,
And how and when and where!"

When you climb up a ladder, you must begin at the bottom, and ascend step by step, until you arrive at the top; and so it is with the principles of the Gospel—you must begin with the first, and go on until you learn all the principles of exaltation. But it will be a great while after you have passed through the veil before you will have learned them. It is not all to be comprehended in this world; it will be a great work to learn our salvation and exaltation even beyond the grave.
—*Joseph Smith.*

The glory of God is intelligence,—*D.&C.* 93:36.

It is impossible for a man to be saved in ignorance.   —*D. & C.* 131:6.

Whatever principle of intelligence we attain
unto in this life, it will rise with us in the resurrection. And if a person gains more knowledge
and intelligence in this life through his diligence
and obedience than another, he will have so much
the advantage in the world to come.

—*D. & C.* 130:18, 19.

"The desire for knowledge, like the thirst for
riches, increases with the acquisition of it."

"Better to weep with the wise than laugh with
the foolish."

Were I so tall to reach the Pole,
    Or grasp the ocean with my span,
I must be measured by my soul:
    The mind's the standard of the man.
                          —*Dr. Watts.*

Teach ye diligently and my grace shall attend you, that you may be instructed more perfectly in theory, in principle, in doctrine, in the law of the gospel, in all things that pertain unto the kingdom of God, that are expedient for you to understand;

Of things both in heaven and in the earth, and under the earth; things which have been, things which are, things which must shortly come to pass; things which are at home, things which are abroad; the wars and the perplexities of the nations, and the judgments which are on the land; and a knowledge also of countries and of kingdoms.   —*D. & C.* 88:78, 79.

A little learning is a dangerous thing;
Drink deep, or taste not the Pierian spring:
There shallow draughts intoxicate the brain,
And drinking largely sobers us again.
                                                            —*Pope.*

Happy is the man that findeth wisdom,
And the man that getteth understanding.
For the merchandise of it is better than the
        merchandise of silver,
And the gain thereof than fine gold.
                                            —*Proverbs* 3:13, 14.

If any of you lack wisdom, let him ask of God, that giveth to all men liberally, and upbraideth not; and it shall be given him.—*James* 1:5.

Wisdom is the principal thing; therefore get wisdom; and with all thy getting get understanding.—*Proverbs* 4:7.

Counsel with the Lord in all thy doings, and he will direct thee for good; yea, when thou liest down at night lie down unto the Lord, that he may watch over you in your sleep; and when thou risest in the morning let thy heart be full of thanks unto God; and if ye do these things, ye shall be lifted up at the last day.—*Alma* 37:37.

When we have received the laying on of hands by those in authority for the gift of the Holy Ghost, we have just received our license to dig for pearls in God's Treasure Field.
—*Dr. W. I. Ghormley.*

The heart is wiser than the intellect.
J. G. Holland.

LIFE AND ITS REWARDS

Life! I know not what thou art,
But know that thou and I must part;
And when, or how, or where we met
I own to me's secret yet.
Life! we've been long together,
Thro' pleasant and thro' cloudy weather;
'Tis hard to part when friends are dear,
Perhaps 'twill cost a sigh, a tear.
   Then steal away—give little warning.
Choose thine own time—
Say not "Good night," but in some brighter
    clime
      Bid me—"Good morning!"
            —*Mrs. Barbauld.*

"Life is a measure to be filled—not a cup to be drained."

Shall he who soars, inspired by loftier views,
Life's little cares and little pains refuse?
Shall he not rather feel a double share
Of mortal woe, when doubly armed to bear?
            —*Crabbe.*

GOD'S WILL FOR YOU AND ME

Just to be tender, just to be true,
Just to be glad the whole day through,
Just to be merciful, just to be mild,
Just to be trustful as a child,
Just to be gentle and kind and sweet,
Just to be helpful with willing feet,
Just to be cheery when things go wrong,
Just to drive sadness away with a song.
Whether the hour is dark or bright,
Just to be loyal to God and right,
Just to believe that God knows best,
Just in His promises ever to rest—
Just to let love be our daily key,
That is God's will for you and me.

—Anonymous.

RIGHT LIVING

Let your food be plain and wholesome
   From all stimulants abstain.
Keep the body you live in
    Clean and pure from every stain.

Let each day be one of doing
   Idle moments are seeds of death.

Strong minds and strong bodies
   require work as well as rest.

Let your mind be chaste and pure
   An evil mind makes vice and crime.
Honest thinking and Noble deeds
   Build a character grand, sublime.

Let each hour be full of sunshine,
   Pleasure comes from doing good.
Life is full of happy moments
   When life's aim is understood.
          —*The Human Culture Digest.*

"Life is not complex if you walk straight."

LIFE INSURANCE

Could I interest you in a policy?
   What kind is it you say?
Well, it's Life Insurance, friend,
   But in a different sort of way.

It's the very same insurance
   That Christ brought to the earth,
And whatever you put into it, friend,
   You'll get your money's worth.

No, you don't pay so much in money
　　As you pay by living right,
Just obey the gospel teachings,
　　And put your sins to flight.

Yes, it pays big dividends,
　　But perhaps not right away;
It insures your "Life Eternal," friend,
　　And you collect on judgment day.

And contrary to worldly ways of man,
　　You the reward will receive;
Invest a lot in this policy, friend,
　　And I promise you shall not grieve.

The Lord will do the collecting, friend,
　　He comes around each day;
And although you cannot see Him,
　　He knows what you do and say.

It's the greatest policy that can be had
　　For it insures the souls of men.
The Gospel of Jesus Christ, my friend,
　　Really pays back in the end.

—Don C. Summers.

"What the future has in store for you depends in large measure on what you place in store for the future."

LIFE AND DEATH

So he died for his faith. That is fine,
  More than most of us do.
But, say, can you add to that line
  That he lived for it too?
In his death he bore witness at last
  As a martyr to the truth.
Did his life do the same in the past,
  From the days of his youth?
It is easy to die. Men have died
  For a wish or a whim—
From bravado or passion or pride,
  Was it harder for him?
But to live—every day to live out
  All the truth that he dreamt,
While his friends met his conduct with doubt
  And the World with contempt.
Was it thus that he plodded ahead,
  Never turning aside?
Then we'll talk of the life that he lived.
  Never mind how he died.

—Ernest Crosby.

"If the end of life is to enjoy life, then we should so live that enjoyment will be possible to the end."

WHAT IS LIFE TO YOU?

To the soldier life's a battle
 To the teacher life's a school.
Life's a "good thing" for the grafter
 It's a failure to the fool.
To the man upon the engine
 Life's a long and heavy grade;
It's a gamble to the gambler;
 To the merchant it's a trade.

Life's a picture to the artist;
 To the rascal life's a fraud;
Life perhaps, is but a burden
 To the man beneath the hod.
Life is lovely to the lover,
 To the player life's a play;
Life may be a load of trouble
 To the man upon the dray.

Life is but a long vacation
 To the man who loves his work.
Life's an everlasting effort
 To the ones who like to shirk.
To the earnest Christian worker
 Life's a story ever new.
Life is what we try to make it,
 Brother, What Is Life to You?
                    —*Anonymous.*

The doctor knows what his trained eyes see
And he says it's the last of the ninth for me.
So once more swing while the clouds loom dark
And then I must leave this noisy park.

'Twas a glorious game from the opening bell—
Good plays, bad plays, thrills pell mell.
The speed of it burned my tears away,
But I thank God that he let me play.
                              —*William F. Kirk.*

There is a law irrevocably decreed in heaven
before the foundations of this world, upon which
all blessings are predicated; and when we obtain any blessing from God it is by obedience **to**
that law upon which it is predicated.
                              —*D. & C.* 130:20.

I, the Lord, am bound when ye do what I say;
but when ye do not what I say, ye have no promise.
                              —*D. & C.* 82:10.

"There are as many lovely things—
    As many pleasant tones
For those who dwell by cottage hearths
    As those who sit on thrones."

LIFE

Struggling, toiling, striving
  Without stress or strife;
Always upward climbing,
  This is the best of life.

Singing, cheering, smiling,
  For miles and miles of life;
Ne'er drooping or pining,
  This is the wine of life.

Serving, helping, giving,
  With a glad spirit rife;
As long as you're living,
  This is the joy of life.

—*Nephi Jensen.*

I have fought a good fight, I have finished my course, I have kept the faith:

Henceforth there is laid up for me a crown of righteousness, which the Lord, the righteous judge, shall give me at that day: and not to me only, but unto all them also that love his appearing.—II *Timothy* 4:7, 8.

Our patriarchal blessings are paragraphs from the book of our possibilities.—*Dr. Maeser.*

I command and men obey not; I revoke and
they receive not the blessing. Then they say in
their hearts: This is not the work of the Lord,
for his promises are not fulfilled. But wo unto
such, for their reward lurketh beneath, and not
from above.   —*D. & C.* 58:32, 33.

LITTLE THINGS

It does not matter if the greatest thing for you
to do be not in itself great. The best prepara-
tion for greatness comes in doing faithfully the
little things that lie nearest. The nearest is the
greatest in most human lives.—*D. S. Jordan.*

I should never have made my success in life if
I had not bestowed upon the least thing I have
ever undertaken, the same attention and care that
I have bestowed upon the greatest.—*Dickens.*

A little folly causeth him who hath reputation
for wisdom and honor to send forth a stinking
savor.—*Eccl.* 10:1.

Great occasions do not make heros or cowards; they only unveil them to the eyes of men. Silently and imperceptibly, as we wake or sleep, we grow strong or weak; and at last some crisis shows us what we have become.—*Cannon Westcot.*

LOVE

Jesus said unto him, Thou shalt love the Lord thy God with all thy heart, and with all thy soul, and with all thy mind.

This is the first and great commandment.

And the second is like unto it, Thou shalt love thy neighbor as thyself.

On these two commandments hang all the law and the prophets.—*Matthew* 22:37-40.

He that saith he is in the light, and hateth his brother is in darkness, even until now.

He that loveth his brother abideth in the light, and there is none occasion of stumbling in him.

But he that hateth his brother is in darkness, and walketh in darkness, and knoweth not whither he goeth, because that darkness hath blinded his eyes.—1 *John* 2:9-11.

I LOVE YOU MOTHER

"I love you, mother," said little John;
   Then forgetting his work, his cap went on,
And he was off to the garden swing,
   Leaving his mother the wood to bring.

"I love you, mother," said little Nell,
   "I love you better than tongue can tell."
Then she teased and pouted half the day,
   Till mother rejoiced when she went to play.

"I love you, mother," said little Nan,
   "Today I'll help you all I can,"
To the cradle then she did softly creep,
   And rocked the baby till he fell asleep.

Then stepping softly, she took the broom
   And swept the floor and dusted the room.
Busy and happy all day was she,
   Helpful and cheerful as child could be.

"I love you, mother," again they said,
   Three little children going to bed.
How do you think the mother guessed
   Which of them really loved her best?

                     —Joy Allison.

He that hath my commandments, and keepeth them, he it is that loveth me: and he that loveth me shall be loved of my Father, and I will love him, and will manifest myself to him.

Judas saith unto him, not Iscariot, Lord, how is it that thou wilt manifest thyself unto us, and not unto the world?

Jesus answered and said unto him, If a man love me, he will keep my words: and my Father will love him, and we will come unto him, and make our abode with him.

He that loveth me not keepeth not my sayings: and the word which ye hear is not mine, but the Father's which sent me.—*John* 14:21-24.

Love is the purification of the heart from self; it strengthens and ennobles the character, gives higher motives and a nobler aim to every action of life, and makes both man and woman strong, noble, and courageous.—*Miss Jewsbury.*

A new commandment I give unto you, That ye love one another; as I have loved you, that ye also love one another.

By this shall all men know that ye are my disciples, if ye have love one to another.

—*John* 13:34-35.

But I say unto you, Love your enemies, bless them that curse you, do good to them that hate you, and pray for them which despitefully use you, and persecute you:

That ye may be the children of your Father which is in heaven, for he maketh his sun to rise on the evil and on the good, and sendeth rain on the just and on the unjust.

For if ye love them which love you, what reward have ye? do not even the publicans the same?

And if ye salute your brethren only, what do ye more than others? do not even the publicans so?

Be ye therefore perfect, even as your Father which is in heaven is perfect.—*Matthew* 5:44-48.

MAN AND MANHOOD

The best man is he who most tries to perfect himself, and the happiest man is he who most feels that he is perfecting himself.—*Socrates.*

Adam fell that men might be; and men are that they might have joy.—II *Nephi* 2:25.

"FOR HONOR AND FOR HER"

Somewhere, a woman, thrusting fear away,
    Faces the future bravely for your sake,
Toils on from dawn till dark, from day to day,
    Fights back her tears, nor heeds the bitter
        ache.
She loves you, trusts you, breathes in prayer your
        name.
    Soil not her faith in you, by sin or shame.

Somewhere, a woman—mother, sweetheart, wife,
    Waits betwixt hopes and fears for your return.
Her kiss, her words, will cheer you in the strife,
    When death itself confronts you, grim and
        stern.
But let her image all your reverence claim,
    When base temptations scorch you with their
        flame.

Somewhere a woman watches, filled with
        pride,
    Shrined in her heart, you share a place with
        none,
She toils, she waits, she prays, till side by side,
    You stand together when the battle's won.
Oh, keep for her dear sake a stainless name,
    Bring back to her a manhood free from
        shame.   *—Margaret Scoutton.*

WANTED

God give us men! A time like this demands
  Strong minds, great hearts, true faith and
    ready hands.
Men whom the lust of lucre does not kill;
  Men whom the spoils of office cannot buy;
Men who possess opinions and a will;
Men who have honor; men who will not lie;
Men who can stand before a demagogue
  And damn his treacherous flatteries without
    winking.

Tall men, sun-crowned, who live above the fog,
  In public duty and in private thinking.
For while the rabble, with their thumb-worn
    creeds,
  Their large professions and their little deeds,
Mingle in selfish strife—lo! Freedom weeps
  Wrong rules the land and waiting Justice
    sleeps.—*J. G. Holland.*

Man is spirit. The elements are eternal, and
spirit and element, inseparably connected, receive
a fullness of joy. And when separated, man cannot receive a fullness of joy.   —*D. & C.* 93:33,34.

THE FOLLOWING WAS WRITTEN IN RESPONSE
TO JOYCE KILMER'S INSPIRING POEM,
"TREES."

Are poets, then, but clownish tools,
And poesy, the sport of fools.
Surely you did not mean it friend,
Forgive me, please, if I offend,
The God who made the lovely tree,
Made poets too, and poetry.
He who fashioned the magic oak,
Through Shakespeare and through Words-
    worth spoke.
He who planted the uptowering pine,
Gave form and force to Milton's line.
Folly's creation! Are they so?
A million voices answer no.
And none among them will decree
That Kilmer was less than Kilmer's tree.
            —*Orson F. Whitney.*

A REAL MAN

Men are of two kinds, and he
Was of the kind I'd like to be.
Some preach their virtues, and a few
Express their lives by what they do
That sort was he. No flowery phrase

Or glibly spoken words of praise
Won friends for him. He wasn't cheap
Or shallow, but his course ran deep,
And it was pure. You know the kind.
Not many in a life you find
Whose deeds outrun their words so far
That more than what they seem they are.

There are two kinds of lies as well:
The kind you live, the ones you tell.
Back through his years from age to youth
He never acted one untruth.
Out in the open light he fought
And didn't care what others thought
Nor what they said about his fight
If he believed that he was right.
The only deeds he ever hid
Was acts of kindness that he did.—*Guest.*

From *Collected Verse of Edgar A. Guest,* copyright 1934, used by permission of The Reilly & Lee Co., Chicago.

WHAT IS MAN?

Man is one of the eternal, imperishable realities of the universe . . . In the beginning, man was with God, a child of God, begotten by Him. He has a divine pedigree.

As a child of God, man partakes of the divine

Nature of his Father. Within him lie germs of infinite development. Potentially he is a Godlike being. Therefore he may rise eternally toward the likeness of his Father in Heaven. Upward, divine, unending, is man's high destiny . . . But progress is ever an inward, not an outward process. His increasing progress is not imposed upon him, salvation is a cooperative enterprise between God and man.

All men are the very children of God. They are brothers. Every man, however humble, of whatever race, has the same origin and possible destiny. . . .

Were this conception, which raises the individual man to immeasurable importance, more fully comprehended, there would come great modification of man's treatment of man. The inhumanity of man to man would soon vanish from the earth. The law of the beast would be replaced by the law of God. Love would triumph over hate. The record of history declares that nations which have recognized in part the true nature of man, have prospered most and survived the longest . . .

A sense of individual responsibility grows out of an understanding of man's relationship to other men and to God. The world is in serious need of a compelling sense of personal, individual, responsibility . . .

To lean upon others for support enfeebles the
soul. By self-effort man will attain his high destiny. It cannot be placed as a cape upon his
shoulders by others. Upon his own feet he must
enter the kingdom of God, whether on earth or in
heaven. By conquest of self he shall win his place
in the everlasting glory of God's presence.

"What is man that thou art mindful of him?"
He is a very son of God, endowed with God-like
power, who, if he respect his divine origin and
high destiny, may bring to pass the long sought
reign of righteousness on earth—*John A. Widtsoe.*

The policy man serves God in such a manner
as not to offend the devil.—*Fuller.*

THE MEASURE OF A MAN

Not—"How did he die?" *But*—"How did he
    live?"
Not—"What did he gain?' *But*—"What did he
    give?"
    These are the units to measure worth
    Of a man as a man regardless of birth.

*   *   *

Not—"What was his station?" *But*—"Had he a
    heart?"
And—"How did he play his God-given part?"

Was he ever ready with a word of good cheer,
To bring back a smile, to banish a tear?

* * *

Not—"What was his church?" *Nor*—"What was
his creed?"
But—"Had he befriended those really in need?"
Not—"What did the sketch in the newspaper say?"
But—"How many were sorry when he passed
away?"   —*Anon.*

A MONKEY'S VIEWPOINT

Three monkeys dining in a cocoanut tree
Were discussing something they thought
shouldn't be,
Said one to the others, "Now, listen, you two—
Here monkeys, is something that cannot be
true:

"That humans descend from our noble race!
Why, it's shocking—a terrible disgrace!
Whoever heard of a monkey deserting his wife;
Leaving a baby to starve; maybe ruin its life?

"And have you ever known of a mother monk
To leave her darling with strangers to bunk?
Human babies are handed from one to another
And some scarcely know the love of a mother.

"I've never known a monkey so selfish to be
As to build a fence 'round a cocoanut tree
So other monkeys couldn't get a wee taste
While bushels of cocoanuts were going to waste.

"Why, if I'd put a fence 'round this cocoanut
    tree,
Starvation would force you to steal food from
    me.
And here is another thing a monkey won't do:
Seek a cocktail parlor and get on a stew;

"Carouse, on a whoopee, disgracing his life,
Then reel madly home and beat up his wife.
Some humans think it fun—they fuss and they
    cuss—
They've descended from something, but it can't
    be from us."—*Anonymous.*

MARRIAGE

The kindest and the happiest pair
Will find occasion to forbear;
And something, ev'ry day they live
To pity, and perhaps forgive.
                 —*Cowper.*

TRIBUTE TO THE TRUE WIFE

Often times I have seen a tall ship glide by against the tide as if drawn by some invisible bowline, with a hundred strong arms pulling. Her sails unfilled, her streamers were drooping, she had neither side wheel nor stern wheel; still she moved on stately, in serene triumph, as with her own life. But I knew that on the other side of the ship, hidden beneath the great bulk that swam so majestically, there was a little toilsome steam tug with a heart of fire and arms of iron, that was tugging it bravely on, and I knew that if the little steam tug untwined her arms and left the ship it would wallow and roll about and drift hither and thither, and go off with the refluent tide, no man knows whither. And so I have known more than one genius, high-decked, full-freighted, idle-sailed, gay-pennoned, but that for the bare toiling arms and brave, warm-beating heart of the faithful little wife that nestles close to him, so that no wind or wave could part them, would have gone down with the stream and have been heard of no more.

—*Oliver Wendell Holmes.*

Whoso forbiddeth to marry is not ordained of God, for marriage is ordained of God unto man.

—*D. & C.* 49:15.

As unto the bow the cord is,
So unto the man is woman;
Though she bends him, she obeys him;
Though she draws him, yet she follows.
Useless each without the other!

—Longfellow.

Marriage is the mother of the world. It preserves kingdoms, and fills cities and churches, and heaven itself.

—Jeremy Taylor.

MERCY

The nearer we get to our Heavenly Father, the more we are disposed to look with compassion on perishing souls; we feel that we want to take them upon our shoulders, and cast their sins behind our backs. If you would have God have mercy on you, have mercy on one another.

—Joseph Smith.

If mercy were not mingled with His power
This wretched world would not subsist an hour.

—Sir W. Davenant.

The quality of mercy is not strained;
It droppeth as the gentle rain from heaven
Upon the place beneath; it is twice blest;
It blesseth him that gives and him that takes,
'Tis mightiest in the mightiest; it becomes
The throned monarch better than his crown;
And earthly power doth then show likest God's
When mercy seasons justice.

—*Shakespeare.*

THE LESSON

She lifted big blue eyes to me,
Brimming with tears,
And in their depths reproach I see,
Unspoken fears.
"Why did you disobey me, child?"
I heard my own voice say;
I saw her quivering lips, and smiled,
And wiped her tears away.

I sinned, and then in suffering paid,
Forgot my God;
But He, through love for me, assuaged
The chastening rod.
"Why didst thou not heed my decree?"
I heard His dear voice say,

"Lift up thy head and look to Me."
Then He wiped my tears away.
—*Mrs. Herman Crady.*

MOTHER

THE BRAVEST BATTLE

The bravest battle that ever was fought,
  Shall I tell you where and when?
On the maps of the world you will find it not,
  'Twas fought by the mothers of men.

Nay, not with a cannon or battle shot,
  With sword or nobler pen,
Nay, not with elegant words or thought
  From mouths of wonderful men.

But deep in a walled-up woman's heart—
  Of woman that would not yield,
But bravely, silently bore her part—
  Lo, there was the battle-field.

No marshalling troops, no bivouac song
  No banner to gleam and wave,
But, O, these battles they last so long,
  From babyhood to the grave!

Yet faithful still as a bridge of stars
   She fights in her walled-up town—
Fights on and on in the endless wars,
   Then silent, unseen—goes down.

O ye with banners and battle shot,
   And soldiers to shout and praise,
I tell you that kingliest victories brought
   Were fought in these silent ways.

O spotless woman in a world of shame,
   With splendid and silent scorn,
Go back to God as white as you came
   The kingliest warrior born.

              —Joaquin Miller.

   They say that man is mighty,
   He governs land and sea,
   He wields a mighty scepter
   O'er lesser powers that be;
   But a mightier power and stronger
   Man from his throne has hurled,
   For the hand that rocks the cradle
   Is the hand that rules the world.
           —Wm. Ross Wallace.

The mother, in her office, holds the key
Of the soul; and she it is who stamps the coin
Of character, and makes the being who would
    be a savage,
But for her gentle cares, a Christian man.
Then crown her Queen o' the world.

                 —Old Play.

OBEDIENCE

If you're told to do a thing,
    And mean to do it really,
Never let it be by halves;
    But do it fully, freely.

Do not make a poor excuse,
    Waiting, weak, unsteady;
All obedience worth the name
    Must be prompt and ready.

                 —Anonymous.

If ye are willing and obedient, ye shall eat of
the good of the land;
  But if ye refuse and rebel, ye shall be devoured
with the sword: for the mouth of the Lord hath
spoken it.   *—Isaiah* 1:19, 20.

My people must needs be chastened until they learn obedience, if it needs be, by the things which they suffer.   —*D. & C.* 105:6.

I, the Lord, am bound when ye do what I say; but when ye do not what I say, ye have no promise.   —*D. & C.* 82:10.

Though he were a Son, yet learned He obedience by the things which he suffered.
                    —*Hebrews* 5:8.

If ye shall be obedient to the commandments, and endure to the end, ye shall be saved at the last day.   —1 *Nephi* 22:31.

Every man receiveth wages of him whom he listeth to obey.   —*Alma* 3:27.

Know ye not, that to whom ye yield yourselves to obey, his servants ye are to whom ye obey; whether of sin unto death, or of obedience unto righteousness.   —*Romans* 6:16.

And Samuel said, Hath God as great delight in burnt offerings and sacrifices, as in obeying the

voice of the Lord? Behold, to obey is better than
sacrifice, and to hearken than the fat of rams.

—1 Samuel 15:22.

Ye shall know the truth, and the truth shall
make you free.   *—John* 8:32.

Only as we learn truth and obey it do we find
freedom and progress.

Obedience to the laws of health frees us from
distress and disease and gives us vigor and comfort
of body.

Obedience to the laws of physics frees us from
cold, darkness and inability and gives us heat,
light and power.

Obedience to the laws of learning frees us
from ignorance and superstition and gives us
knowledge and wisdom.

Obedience to the laws of society would free
us from strife and contention and give us peace
and harmonious living.

Obedience to the laws of the gospel would free
us from the grasp of the evil one and give us
salvation and exaltation.

Obedience to the laws of God would free us
from all opposing powers and give us joy in-
expressible and eternal.   *—E.L.M.*

OPPORTUNITY

There is a tide in the affairs of men, which, taken at the flood, leads on to fortune; omitted, all the voyage of their life is bound in shallows and in miseries.—*Shakespeare.*

I expect to pass through this world but once. Any good work, therefore, any kindness, or any service I can render to any soul of man or animal, let me do it now! Let me not neglect or defer it, for I shall not pass this way again.—*Carlyle.*

Eagerness to earn bread and butter has overshadowed many a golden opportunity.—*Maeser.*

LIFE'S LESSON

Learn to make the most of life,
  Lose no happy day,
Time can never bring thee back
  Chances swept away.

Leave no tender word unsaid,
  Love while life shall last,
The mill will never turn again
  With water that has past.
    —*Anonymous.*

I SHALL NOT PASS AGAIN THIS WAY

The bread that bringeth strength I want to give,
The water pure that bids the thirsty live;
I want to help the fainting day by day;
I'm sure I shall not pass again this way.

I want to give the oil of joy for fears,
The faith to conquer crowding doubts and fears.
Beauty for ashes may I give alway;
I'm sure I shall not pass again this way;

I want to give good measure running o'er,
And into angry hearts I want to pour
The answer soft that turneth wrath away;
I'm sure I shall not pass again this way.

I want to give to others, hope and faith,
I want to do all that the Master saith;
I want to live aright from day to day
I'm sure I shall not pass again this way.

—W. R. Fitch.

The wise man will make more opportunities than he finds.—*Bacon.*

OPPORTUNITY PASSING

Master of human destinies am I;
Fame, love and fortune on my foot-steps wait.
Cities and fields I walk; I penetrate
Deserts and seas remote, and, passing by
Hovel and mart and palace, soon or late
I knock, unbidden, once on every gate.
If sleeping, awake; if feasting, rise before
I turn away. It is the hour of fate,
And they who follow me reach every state
Mortals desire, and conquer every foe
Save death. But those who doubt or hesitate,
Condemned to failure, penury and woe,
Seek me in vain and needlessly implore;
I answer not and I return no more.

—J. J. Ingalls.

The greatest opportunity of life is life itself. Here and now is your chance and mine to make for ourselves the kind of life we would like to live forever. Far greater grandeur and magnificence than the mind can conceive; peace, joy and soulful satisfaction far beyond the power of man to measure is ours now to provide. In a short life here to make happiness for a long life hereafter is our present opportunity.—*E. L. M.*

PARENTS

FATHER'S FOOTSTEPS

A father and his tiny son
  Crossed a rough street one stormy day.
"See, papa," cried the little one,
  "I stepped in your steps all the way."

Ah, random childish hands that deal
  Quick thrusts no coat of steel could stay;
It touched him with the touch of steel:
  "I stepped in your steps all the way."

If this man shirks his manhood due,
  And heeds what lying voices say;
It is not one who falls, but two—
  "I stepped in your steps all the way."

But they who thrust off greed and fear,
  Who love and watch, who toil and pray;
How their hearts carol when they hear,
  "I stepped in your steps all the way."

                                    —*Anonymous.*

THOROUGHBREDS

You talk of your breed of cattle
  And plan for a higher strain,
You double the food of your pasture
  And heap up the measures of grain;
You draw on the wits of the nation
  To better the barn and the pen;
But what are you doing, my brothers
  To better the breed of Men?

You boast of your Morgans and Herefords,
  Of the worth of a calf or a colt.
And scoff at the scrub and the mongrel
  As worthy the fool or the dolt;
You mention the points of your roadster
  With many a "wherefore" and "when,"
But, ah, are you counting, my brothers,
  The worth of the children of Men?

And what of your boy? Have you measured
  His needs for a growng year?
Does your mark as his sire, in his features
  Mean less than the brand on your steer?
Thoroughbred! That is your watchword
  For stable and pasture and pen;
But what is your word for the homestead?
  Answer, you brothers of men!

—*Rose Trumbell.*

Inasmuch as parents have children in Zion . . . that teach them not to understand the doctrine of repentance, faith in Christ the Son of the living God, and of baptism and the gift of the Holy Ghost, by the laying on of hands, when eight years old, the sin be upon the heads of the parents.—*D. & C.* 68:25.

PATIENCE

Just why I suffer loss I cannot know,
I only know my Father wills it so.
He leads in paths I cannot understand;
But all the way I know is wisely planned.
My life is only mine that I may use
The gifts He lendeth me as He may choose;
And if in love some boon He does recall,
I know that unto Him belongeth all.
I am His child and I can safely trust;
He loves me and I know that He is just.
Within His love I can securely rest,
Assured that what he does for me is best.
                    —*Edith Virginia Eradt.*

Patience is a necessary ingredient of genius.
                    —*Benj. Disraeli.*

To man it seemed that evil had prevailed,
That His fair life had altogether failed,
And nought was left but what the cross im-
    paled—
  But God saw otherwise!

We too, at times, come nigh to lose our hope,
When with life's evils we no more can cope,
And in the dark with heavy hearts we grope;
  But God sees otherwise.—*Anonymous.*

Every man must patiently bide his time. He
must wait—not in listless idleness—but in constant, steady, cheerful endeavors, always willing
and fulfilling and accomplishing his task, that
when the occasion comes he may be equal to the
occasion.—*Longfellow.*

Patience and determination will win for most
of us nine battles out of ten. A man without patience is a lamp without oil.—*de Musset.*

"Patience is waiting. Not passively waiting.
That is laziness. But to keep going when the
going is hard and slow—that is patience."

To endure is greater than to dare.—*Thackeray.*

PEACE

For I am no respecter of persons, and will that all men shall know that the day speedily cometh; the hour is not yet, (1831) but is nigh at hand, when peace shall be taken from the earth and the devil shall have power over his own dominion.

—*D. & C.* 1:35.

Blessed are the peacemakers; for they shall be called the children of God.—*Matthew* 5:9.

Peace I leave with you, my peace I give unto you; not as the world giveth, give I unto you. Let not your heart be troubled, neither let it be afraid. —*John* 14:27.

REPOSE

When hands join hands around the world,
　To form the friendship chain of peace,
The flag of love will be unfurled
　And aching hearts will find release.
　　　　　—*Remelda Nielsen Gibson.*

Peace above all things is to be desired; but blood must sometimes be spilled to obtain it on equable and lasting terms.—*Andrew Jackson.*

These things I have spoken unto you, that in me ye might have peace. In the world ye shall have tribulation; but be of good cheer; I have overcome the world.—*John* 16:33.

Arming a country with guns and tanks and airplanes is not enough. If our defense program is to succeed, the entire country must experience a rebirth, for in the end, only righteousness can save a nation.—*Roger W. Babson.*

PRAYER

"Prayer is the passport to spiritual power."

So weak is man—so ignorant and blind, that did not God sometimes withhold in mercy what we ask, we should be ruined at our own request.
—*Hannah More.*

After this manner therefore pray ye: Our Father which art in heaven, Hallowed be thy name.

Thy kingdom come, Thy will be done in earth, as it is in heaven.

Give us this day our daily bread:

And forgive us our debts, as we forgive our debtors.

And lead us not into temptation, but deliver us from evil: For thine is the kingdom, and the power, and the glory, for ever. Amen.

—Matthew 6:9-13.

All our prayers are addressed in the handwriting of the heart, readable to God and ourselves only.—*Dr. Maeser.*

> O Thou from Whom all goodness flows,
>   I lift my heart to Thee:
> In all my sorrows, conflicts, woes,
>   Good Lord, remember me.—*Anon.*

> Speak to Him thou, for He hears
>   And spirit with spirit may meet
> Closer is He than breathing
>   And nearer than hands and feet.
>   *—Tennyson.*

So long I have been guided by thy power,
　　Up many a tangled path and stony hill;
And now, dear Lord, through this strange,
　　　　darkened hour,
　　Be with me still.

Be with me for the way is long and lonely—
　　I am bewildered and I cannot see;
But Lord, I shall not be afraid, if only
　　Thou wilt walk with me.

If only I can some way keep recalling
　　The darkened roads I traveled in the past,
How, after Thou didst long guard me from
　　　　falling,
　　Light shone at last.

Then surely, Lord, I can go forward, knowing
　　That somewhere on the hills the light will
　　　　dawn,
And I shall reach it safely, if in going
　　Thou wilt still lead on.
　　　　　　　　　　　　—*Grace Noll Crowell.*

　　He prayeth best, who loveth best
　　　　All things both great and small;
　　For the dear God who loveth us,
　　　　He made and loveth all.
　　　　　　　　　　　　—*Coleridge.*

IF I BUT PRAY

When noises in the still of night
Fill my heart with dread and fright
I feel more calm, when thoughts recite:
"God will protect you. Do what's right."

When I feel want and deep despair
And need God most, I know he's there
Within my reach, if I but pray,
And give him thanks from day to day.

And when life's trials pass my way,
They grow much lighter when I pray.
I've many blessings in reserve,
God gives me more than I deserve!

—Remelda Nielsen Gibson.

Father let my voice be heard,
Not in anger rashly stirred.
Bless thy children whom I meet.
Let thy Gospel keep them sweet,
As I travel forth each day,
Be thou with me all the way.
Good to others let me do;
Virtue, peace, and joy pursue.

—T. R. Bray.

A PRAYER

Lord, keep my heart from breaking,
    Though life robs me of my all;
Let me know that Thou art waiting,
    Ever near me when I call.

Lord, let not my heart grow bitter,
    Though in sorrow I must walk;
Let me look beyond the shadows,
    Make me deaf when others mock.
                —Arilla B. Wilson.

ANSWER TO PRAYER

We ask for strength and God gives us
    difficulties which make us strong.
We pray for wisdom and God sends us problems,
    the solution of which develops wisdom.
We plead for prosperity and God gives
    us brain and brawn to work.
We plead for courage and God gives
    us dangers to overcome.
We ask for favors—God gives us
    opportunities.
        This is the answer.
                —Hugh B. Brown.

Prayer is a force as real as terrestrial gravity. As a physician I have seen men, after all other therapy had failed, lifted out of disease and melancholy by the serene effort of prayer. It is the only power in the world that seems to overcome the so-called "laws of nature." The occasions on which prayer has dramatically done this have been termed "miracles." But a constant quieter miracle takes place hourly in the hearts of men and women who have discovered that prayer supplies them with a steady flow of sustaining power in their daily lives.

—*Alexis Carrel, M.D.*

Prayer is the soul's sincere desire
   Uttered or unexpressed;
The motion of a hidden fire
   That trembles in the breast.

Prayer is the simplest form of speech
   That infant lips can try;
Prayer, the sublimest strains that reach
   The Majesty on high.

O Thou by whom we come to God—
   The Life, the Truth, the Way!
The path of prayer Thyself hast trod;
   Lord, teach us how to pray.

—*Montgomery.*

HYMN TO SERVICE

O Lord, our Helper, strong, we plead
For mercy as we pray;
Thy word we ask to meet each need,
Thy grace for that blessed day
When Israel's hosts their God shall meet
Kneeling in meekness at His feet.

May we, O Father, ever know
Thy sweet, abiding grace;
May love and faith together grow
And every fault efface;
In mercy may our hearts be led
To bless the living and the dead.

Make strong our ranks in every land,
Each race and tongue unite;
With Thine anointed sons we stand
Courageous for the right.
High may our songs of peace now ring
To hail the triumph of our King.

—*C. Frank Steele.*

My words fly up; my thoughts remain below.
Words without thoughts never to heaven go.

—*Shakespeare.*

PRIESTHOOD

———

Bearers of the Priesthood: "Your ordination to the Priesthood is an officer's commission in the army of the Lord.

"No longer are you a mere soldier, but a captain of salvation, with not only the duty to obey all commands, but with the responsibility of bravely leading others."

When men are called unto mine everlasting gospel, and covenant with an everlasting covenant, they are accounted as the salt of the earth and the savor of men.

They are called to be the savor of men; therefore, if that salt of the earth lose its savor, behold it is thenceforth good for nothing only to be cast out and trodden under the feet of men.

—*D. & C.* 101:39, 40.

"You are playing for a big stake—the approval of the Lord—and unessentials should not disturb."

Wherefore now, let every man learn his duty, and to act in the office in which he is appointed, in all diligence.

He that is slothful shall not be counted worthy to stand, and he that learns not his duty and shows himself not approved shall not be counted worthy to stand.—*D. & C.* 107:99-100.

PROGRESS

Shall we not continue on to perfection after the resurrection? Is not the promise given that we shall, if faithful in all things, become *like* Jesus Christ and the Father?

"Behold, what manner of love the Father hath bestowed upon us, that we should be called the sons of God; therefore, the world knoweth us not, because it knew him not. Beloved, *now* are we the sons of God, and it doth not yet appear what we shall be; but we know that, when he shall appear, *we shall be like him;* for we shall see him as he is. And every man that hath this hope in him purifieth himself, even as he is pure." (1 John 3:1-3).—*Joseph Fielding Smith, in "The Way to Perfection."*

So pleased at first the tow'ring Alps to try,
We mount o'er the vales, and seem to tread the
   sky;
The eternal snows appear already past,
And the first clouds and mountains seem the
   last,
But, those attained, we tremble to survey
The growing labors of the lengthened way.
The increasing prospect tires our wand'ring eyes,
Hills peep o'er hills, and Alps on Alps arise!
                         —*Alexander Pope.*

PURITY

When a person tells an unclean story he imbeds
impurity deeper in his own mind; he breaks down
his own resistance to evil; he talks himself into the
idea that the smutty thing he talks about isn't so
bad after all, and he narrows the breach between
the unclean thought and the unclean deed. He
sets up an acceptance in his own mind of the
type of filth he discusses and lays a foundation
for sinful acts. He builds a barrier against his
own reception of the Spirit of God and its guid-
ance.   —*Church News, Editorial.*

Purity in person and in morals is true godliness—*Hosea Ballou.*

IT'S A POOR JOKE

When some woman blushes with embarrassment.

When some heart carries away an ache.

When something sacred is made to appear common.

When a man's weakness provides the cause for laughter.

When profanity is required to make it funny.

When a little child is brought to tears.

When everyone can't join in the laughter.

—*Exchange.*

I pray Thee, O God, that I may be beautiful within.—*Socrates.*

Know ye not that ye are the temple of God, and that the Spirit of God dwelleth in you?

If any man defile the temple of God, him shall God destroy; for the temple of God is holy, which temple ye are.—*1 Cor.* 3:16, 17.

RECORDS

And I saw the dead, small and great, stand before God; and the books were opened: and another book was opened, which is the book of life; and the dead were judged out of those things which were written in the books, according to their works.

And the sea gave up the dead which were in it; and death and hell delivered up the dead which were in them: and they were judged every man according to their works.—*Revelation* 20:12, 13.

Whate'er you say, whate'er you do,
   Be it for shame or enduring glory;
From your cradle days to the end of life,
   You're writing your life's secret story.

Each month ends a thirty-page chapter,
   Each year means the end of a part,
And never an act is misstated,
   Nor ever one wish of the heart.

Each day when you wake, the book opens
   Revealing a page clean and white.
What thoughts and what words and what doings
   Will cover its surface by night?

God leaves that to you, you're the writer,
 And never one word shall grow dim;
Till some day you write the word "finis,"
 And give back your life book to Him.
     —Adrian Klinger.

IT SHOWS IN YOUR FACE

You don't have to tell how you live each day;
You don't have to say if you work or you play;
A tried, true barometer serves in the place,
However you live, it will show in your face.
The false, the deceit that you bear in your heart
Will not stay inside where it first got a start;
For sinew and blood are a thin veil of lace—
What you wear in your heart, you wear in your
   face.
If your life is unselfish, if for others you live.
For not what you get, but how much you can
   give;
If you live close to God in His infinite grace—
You don't have to tell it, it shows in your face.
     —Anonymous.

Every thought, every word, every deed makes its
record on the tablets of the soul. That record is
an undeniable picture of what we are.—*E. L. M.*

RELIGION

Men must be governed by God, or they will be ruled by tyrants.—*William Penn.*

Wherewith shall I come before the Lord,
And bow myself before the high God?
Shall I come before him with burnt offerings,
With calves of a year old?
Will the Lord be pleased with thousands of
    rams,
Or with ten thousands of rivers of oil?
Shall I give my first born for my transgression,
The fruit of my body for the sin of my soul?
He hath shewed thee, O man, what is good;
And what doth the Lord require of thee,
But to do justly, and to love mercy,
And to walk humbly with thy God?
                          —*Micah*, 6:6-8.

You may discover tribes of men without police or laws, or cities, or any of the arts of life; but nowhere will you find them without some form of religion.—*Blair.*

If any man among you seem to be religious, and bridleth not his tongue, but deceiveth his own heart, this man's religion is vain.

Pure religion and undefiled before God and the Father, is this, To visit the fatherless and widows in their affliction, and to keep himself unspotted from the world.—*James* 1:26, 27.

"Beecher affirmed that all the theology which he ever preached in Plymouth pulpit might be expressed in one brief paragraph: 'There are two natures in every man, the higher and the lower, the physical and the spiritual, and religion consists in bringing the lower into subjection to the higher.'"

It is the property of the religious spirit to be the most refining of all influences. No external advantages, no culture of the tastes, no habit of command, no association with the elegant, or even depth of affection, can bestow that delicacy and that grandeur of bearing which belong only to the mind accustomed to celestial conversation. All else is but gilt and cosmetics.—*Emerson.*

Religious contention is the devil's harvest.
—*La Fontaine.*

REPENTANCE

"There is no pleasure in life equal to that of the conquest of a vicious habit."

Therefore I command you to repent—repent, lest I smite you by the rod of my mouth, and by my wrath, and by my anger, and your sufferings be sore—how sore you know not, how exquisite you know not, yea, how hard to bear you know not.

For behold, I, God, have suffered these things for all, that they might not suffer if they would repent;

But if they would not repent they must suffer even as I.—*D. & C.* 19:15-17.

For I the Lord cannot look upon sin with the least degree of allowance;

Nevertheless, he that repents and does the commands of the Lord shall be forgiven;

And he that repents not, from him shall be taken even the light which he has received; for my Spirit shall not always strive with man, saith the Lord of Hosts.—*D. & C.* 1:31-33.

Of all acts is not repentance most divine?
The greatest of faults is to be conscious of none.
—*Carlyle.*

It is not men's faults that ruin them, so much as the manner in which they conduct themselves after the faults have been committed. The wise will profit by the suffering they cause and eschew them in the future. But there are those on whom experience exerts no ripening influence, who only grow narrower and bitterer and more vicious with time.—*Samuel Smiles.*

Ye cannot say, when ye are brought to that awful crisis, that I will repent, that I will return to my God. Nay, ye cannot say this; for that same spirit which doth possess your bodies at the time that ye go out of this life, that same spirit will have power to possess your body in that eternal world.
—*B. of M., Alma* 34:34.

Repentance becomes more difficult as the sin is more wilful; . . . As the time of repentance is procrastinated, the ability to repent grows weaker; neglect of opportunity in holy things brings a forfeit of the chance.

—*Dr. James E. Talmage.*

RESPONSIBILITY

Responsibility walks hand in hand with capacity and power.—*J. G. Holland.*

IT'S YOU

If you want to work for the kind of a branch
Like the kind of a branch you like,
You needn't slip your clothes in a grip,
Or start on a long, long hike.
You'll only find what you left behind
For there's nothing that's really new.
It's a knock at yourself when you knock your
    branch.
It isn't the branch—it's you.

Real branches are not made by men afraid,
Lest somebody else gets ahead,
When everyone works, and nobody shirks,
You can raise a branch that's dead,
And if while you make your personal stake
Your neighbor can make one, too,
Your branch will be what you want it to be.
It isn't the branch—it's you.

—From "Ka Elele O Hawaii."

AS I GO ON MY WAY

My life shall touch a dozen lives
   Before this year is done,
Make countless marks for good or ill,
   Ere sets the evening sun.
So this is the thought I always think,
   The prayer I always pray:
"Lord, may my life bless other lives
   It touches by the way."
              —Gillilan.

"I know that each sinful action,
   As sure as sunshine follows shade,
Is somewhere, sometime punished,
   Though the hour be long delayed."

"All men have the God-given right to think and believe as they will, and all men have the God-given responsibility to render an accounting sometime, somewhere, for those things which they choose to think and believe."—*Richard L. Evans.*

There is no sort of wrong deed for which a man can bear the punishment alone.
              —George Eliot.

"NOBODY'S BUSINESS BUT MINE"

"A young man is father of five children, oldest four years old, wife just out of hospital with twins. He is sued, judgment secured and wages garnisheed, for recovery on charges in a bastard case of twelve years ago. Who pays?"

HOW MANY HURT?

"Suppose," said I, "You chanced to see
A small boy tumble from a tree,
How would you tell that tale to me?"

"Why, Dad," said he, "I'd simply say
I saw a boy get hurt today
And two men carried him away."

"How many injured would there be?"
I asked. "Just one, of course," said he
"The boy who tumbled from the tree."

"No, no," I answered him, "That fall
Which hurt the lad, brought pain to all
Who knew and loved that youngster small.

"His mother wept, his father sighed,
His brothers and his sisters cried,
And all his friends were hurt inside.

"Remember this your whole life through—
Whatever hurts may come to you
Must hurt all who love you, too.

"You cannot live your life alone,
We suffer with your slightest groan,
And make your pain or grief our own.

"If you should do one shameful thing,
You could not bear alone the sting,
We'd spend our years in suffering.

"How many hurt, we cannot state,
There never falls a blow of fate,
But countless people feel its weight."
                    —*From "The Foreman."*

RICHES

Lay not up for yourselves treasures upon earth,
where moth and rust doth corrupt, and where
thieves break through and steal:

But lay up for yourselves treasures in heaven,
where neither moth nor rust doth corrupt, and
where thieves do not break through nor steal:

For where your treasure is, there will your
heart be also.—*Matthew* 6:19-21.

Wo unto you rich men, that will not give your substance to the poor, for your riches will canker your souls; and this shall be your lamentation in the day of visitation, and of judgment, and of indignation: The harvest is past, the summer is ended, and my soul is not saved!

Wo unto you poor men, whose hearts are not broken, whose spirits are not contrite, and whose bellies are not satisfied, and whose hands are not stayed from laying hold upon other men's goods, whose eyes are full of greediness and who will not labor with your own hands!

But blessed are the poor who are pure in heart, whose hearts are broken, and whose spirits are contrite, for they shall see the kingdom of God coming in power and great glory unto their deliverance; for the fatness of the earth shall be theirs.

For behold, the Lord shall come, and his recompense shall be with him, and he shall reward every man, and the poor shall rejoice;

And their generations shall inherit the earth from generation to generation, forever and ever.

—*D. & C.* 56:16-20.

"Wealth is not his who gets it; but his who enjoys it."

Then said Jesus unto his disciples, If any man will come after me, let him deny himself, and take up his cross, and follow me.

For whosoever will save his life shall lose it: and whosoever will lose his life for my sake shall find it.

For what is a man profited, if he shall gain the whole world, and lose his own soul? or what shall a man give in exchange for his soul?

—*Matthew* 16:24-26.

For the earth is full, and there is enough and to spare; yea, I prepared all things, and have given unto the children of men to be agents unto themselves.

Therefore, if any man shall take of the abundance which I have made, and impart not his portion, according to the law of my gospel, unto the poor and the needy, he shall, with the wicked, lift up his eyes in hell, being in torment.

—*D. & C.* 104:17, 18.

He is the rich man who can avail himself of other men's faculties—who knows how to draw a benefit from the labors and experience of other men.—*Emerson.*

And he said unto them, Take heed, and beware of covetousness for a man's life consisteth not in the abundance of the things which he possesseth.

And he spake a parable unto them, saying, The ground of a certain rich man brought forth plentifully:

And he thought within himself, saying, What shall I do, because I have no room where to bestow my fruits?

And he said, This will I do: I will pull down my barns, and build greater; and there will I bestow all my fruits and my goods.

And I will say to my soul, Soul, thou hast much goods, laid up for many years; take thine ease, eat, drink, and be merry.

But God said unto him, Thou fool! this night thy soul shall be required of thee: then whose shall those things be, which thou hast provided?

So is he that layeth up treasure for himself, and is not rich toward God.—*Luke* 12:15-21.

It's good to have money and the things that money can buy, but it's good, too, to check up once in a while and make sure you haven't lost the things that money can't buy.

—George Horace Latimer.

Seek not for riches but for wisdom; and, behold, the mysteries of God shall be unfolded unto you, and then shall you be made rich. Behold, he that hath eternal life is rich.—*D. & C.* 11:7.

SABBATH

A sabbath well spent
Brings a week of content
    And health for the joys of tomorrow.
But a Sabbath profaned
Whatever be gained
    Is a sure forerunner of sorrow.

—*Matthew Hale.*

And that thou mayest more fully keep thyself unspotted from the world, thou shalt go to the house of prayer and offer up thy sacraments upon my holy day; For verily this is a day appointed unto you to rest from your labors, and to pay thy devotions unto the Most High.—*D. & C.* 59:9, 10.

Six days shalt thou labor and do all thy work;
But the seventh day is the Sabbath of the Lord
thy God; in it thou shalt not do any work.

—Exodus 20:9, 10.

SERVICE

There is a destiny that makes us brothers;
    None goes his way alone;
All that we send into the lives of others
    Comes back into our own.

—Edwin Markham.

What do we live for if not to make life less
difficult for others?

—George Eliot.

Now behold, a marvelous work is about to come
forth among the children of men.

Therefore, O ye that embark in the service of
God, see that ye serve him with all your heart,
might, mind and strength, that ye may stand
blameless before God at the last day.

—D. & C. 4:1, 2.

THE LORD'S JOB

The Lord one day had a job for me,
  But I had so much to do;
So I said, "Please Lord, get somebody else,
  Or, wait till I get through."
I don't know how the Lord came out,
  But He seemed to get along;
But I felt a kind of sneaking like,
  And knowed I'd done Him wrong.

One day I needed the Lord myself,
  Needed Him right away;
But He never answered me at all—
  But yet I could hear Him say,
Away down in my accusing heart,
  "I've got so much to do—
You get somebody else this time,
  Or wait till I get through."

Now when the Lord has a job for me,
  I never try to shirk;
I drop whatever I have on hand,
  And do the good Lord's work.
And my affairs can run along,
  Or wait till I get through;
For nobody else can do the job
  That the Lord marked out for you.
                    —*Paul L. Dunbar.*

And whosoever will be chief among you, let
him be your servant.—*Matt.* 20:27.

If we can be with faithless men who say,
"There is no God—no higher power than mine;"
And still not lose our faith in Him who sent
His Son to give us knowledge—truth divine;

If we can render charity and peace,
To those who suffer mind or body pain,
And comfort those whose mourning does not cease,
Our efforts here shall not have been in vain.

                —Virginia Christopherson.

The race of mankind would perish did they
cease to aid each other. From the time that the
mother binds the child's head, till the moment
that some kind assistant wipes the death-damp
from the brow of the dying, we cannot exist without mutual help. All, therefore, that need aid
have a right to ask it from their fellow-mortals;
no one who holds the power of granting can refuse it without guilt.

                      —Walter Scott.

He doeth well who doeth good
To those of his own brotherhood;
He doeth better who doth bless
The stranger in his wretchedness;
Yet best, oh! best of all doth he
Who helps a fallen enemy.

—Unknown

SELF-CONTROL

The first and best victory is to conquer self; to be conquered by self is of all things most shameful and vile.—*Plato*

The lives of men who have been always growing are strewed along their whole course with the things they have learned to do without.

—Phillips Brooks.

"Self-control is the only sure evidence of personal courage; it is the only means through which personal powers of endurance and thought may be centered upon any object; it is the only possible way to maintain confidence and secure the confidence of one's group."—*C.M.C.*

Let your needs rule you—pamper them and you will see them multiply like insects in the sun. The more you give them the more they demand.

—*Wagner.*

It is easier to suppress the first desire than to satisfy all that follow it.

—*Benjamin Franklin.*

SCHOOL THY FEELINGS, O MY BROTHER

School thy feelings, O my brother,
   Train thy warm, impulsive soul,
Do not its emotions smother,
   But let wisdom's voice control.

School thy feelings, there is power
   In the cool, collected mind;
Passion shatters reason's tower,
   Makes the clearest vision blind
School thy feelings, condemnation
   Never pass on friend or foe,
Though the tide of accusation
   Like a flood of truth may flow

Hear defense before deciding,
    And a ray of light may gleam,
Showing thee what filth is hiding
    Underneath the shallow stream.

Should affliction's acrid vial
    Burst o'er thy unsheltered head,
School thy feelings to the trial,
    Half its bitterness hath fled.
                —*Charles W. Penrose.*

SIN

What maintains one vice would bring up two
children.—*Benjamin Franklin.*

He who finds pleasure in vice and pain in
virtue, is still a novice in both.—*Chinese Proverb.*

Vice is a monster of so frightful mien
As to be hated, needs but to be seen;
Yet seen too oft, familiar with her face,
We first endure, then pity, then embrace.
                —*Pope.*

Would you judge of the lawfulness or the unlawfulness of a pleasure, take this rule. Whatever weakens your reason, impairs the tenderness of your conscience, obscures your sense of God, or takes off the relish of spiritual things; whatever increases the authority of your body over your mind—that thing, to you, is sin.

—John Wesley's Mother.

The wages of sin is death.—*Rom.* 6:23.

The way of transgressors is hard.

—Proverbs 13:15.

'Tis easier work if we begin
  To fear the Lord betimes;
While sinners, that grow old in sin.
  Are hardened in their crimes.

—Isaac Watts.

Sin first is pleasing, then it grows easy, then delightful, then frequent, then habitual, then confirmed; then the man is impenitent, then he is obstinate, then he is resolved never to repent, and then he is ruined.—*Leighton.*

SINCERITY

Thou must be true to thyself if thou the
    truth would teach
Thy soul must overflow, if thou another's
    soul would reach.
It needs the overflow of heart to give the
    lips full speech.—*Boner.*

Sincerity is religion personified.—*Chapin.*

"The only conclusive evidence of a man's sincerity is that he gives himself for a principle. Words, money, all things else, are comparatively easy to give away; but when a man makes a gift of his daily life and practice, it is plain that the truth, whatever it may be, has taken possession of him."—*Lowell.*

Sincerity is to speak as we think, to do as we pretend and profess, to perform and make good what we promise, and really to be what we would seem and appear to be.—*Tillotson.*

SOWING

Be not deceived: God is not mocked; for whatsoever a man soweth, that shall he also reap.

For he that soweth to his flesh, shall of the flesh reap corruption; but he that soweth to the Spirit, shall of the Spirit reap life everlasting.

And let us not be weary in well doing; for in due season we shall reap, if we faint not.

—Gal. 6:7-9.

The wild oats we sow sprout early and grow fast and soon send their roots into the spinal column, until by and by we find ourselves grown through and through.—*Anon.*

The ladder to eternal life is bathed in blood and
    tears;
But joy and happiness await the ones who climb
    it through the years.
Day by day, deed by deed; the way made easier as
    they go,
New strength is theirs, new will, new hope—
The seeds they reap are those they sow.

—T. R. Bray.

We are sowing, daily sowing
  Countless seeds of good and ill
Scattered on the level lowland,
  Cast upon the windy hill;

By a whisper sow we blessings,
  By a breath we scatter strife,
In our words, and looks, and actions
  Lie the seeds of death and life.
          —*H. A. Tuckett.*

SPIRITUALITY

Men of worldly attitude complain that spiritual matters belong to the mystic realms of unreality. They cannot seem to realize that spiritual light and understanding come only as we comply with the laws that control. As the muscles of the body grow strong only by use, so we can become spiritually strong only as we exercise our spiritual powers. In the fields of science these men are willing to start at the bottom and study upward; but in the realms of the spiritual they complain because they cannot understand the problems of trigonometry and calculus when they have not mastered the rudiments of arithmetic.—*E. L. M.*

For what man knoweth the things of a man, save the spirit of man which is in him? Even so the things of God knoweth no man, but the Spirit of God.—1 *Cor.* 2:11.

CERTITUDES

I cannot see the far off starlit scene
  That the outside curtains of space confine,
But when my spirit is fine and serene
  I can see the infinite smile benign.

I do not know how suns were wrought from dust
  By the cosmic power's eternal swirl,
But when I look up and sincerely trust,
  My soul finds rest in life's maddening whirl.

I cannot measure time's unending way
  Or gauge its dizzy sweep o'er star and sod,
But when Christ's spirit in my heart holds sway
  I feel the ever beating heart of God.
                —Nephi Jensen.

Behold, I stand at the door and knock; if any man hear my voice, and open the door, I will come into him and will sup with him and he with me.
                —Rev. 3:20.

Trust no one to be your teacher nor your minister except he be a man of God; walking in his ways and keeping his commandments.

—*B. of M., Mosiah* 23:14.

"If you will pull up a doubt you will generally find a sin at the root of it."

If wrinkles must be written upon the brow, let them not be written upon the heart. The spirit should never grow old.

—*James A. Garfield.*

Martha, Martha, thou are careful and troubled about many things; but one thing is needful; and Mary has chosen that good part, which shall not be taken away from her.—*Luke* 10:41, 42.

The life is more than meat, and the body more than raiment.—*Luke* 12:23.

Mormonism teaches that men do not walk alone. There are always among us personages and forces from the greater, unseen world, which has ultimate direction of the visible world.

—*Dr. John A. Widtsoe.*

SUCCESS

However things may seem, no evil thing is success and no good thing is failure.—*Longfellow*.

THE SUCCESS FAMILY

The father of Success is Work.

The mother of Success is Ambition.

The oldest son is Common Sense.

Some of the other boys are: Perseverance, Honesty, Thoroughness, Foresight, Enthusiasm, Co-operation.

The oldest daughter is Character.

Some of the sisters are: Cheerfulness, Loyalty, Courtesy, Care, Economy, Sincerity, Harmony.

The baby is Opportunity.

Get acquainted with the "old man" and you will be able to get along pretty well with the rest of the family.—*Anonymous*.

Success is never found on top of the hill if the duties at the foot are neglected.

—Eva Arrington.

WHAT IS SUCCESS?

It's doing your work the best you can,
And being just to your fellow man;
It's making money, but holding friends,
And staying true to your aims and ends;
It's figuring how and learning why,
And looking forward and thinking high,
And dreaming a little and doing much;
It's keeping always in closest touch
With what is finest in word and deed;
It's being thorough, yet making speed;
It's daring blithely the field of chance
While making labor a brave romance.
It's going onward despite defeat,
And fighting staunchly, but keeping sweet;
It's being clean and it's playing fair;
It's laughing lightly at Dame Despair;
It's looking up to the stars above,
And drinking deeply of life and love;
It's struggling on with the will to win,
But taking loss with a cheerful grin;
It's sharing sorrow, and work, and mirth,
And making better this good old earth;
It's serving, striving, through strain and stress;
It's doing your noblest—that's success.

—Anonymous.

TEN COMMANDMENTS OF SUCCESS

1. Work Hard. Hard work is the best investment a man can make.

2. Study Hard. Knowledge enables a man to work more intelligently and effectively.

3. Have Initiative. Ruts often deepen into graves.

4. Love Your Work. Then you will find pleasure in mastering it.

5. Be Exact. Slipshod methods bring only slipshod results.

6. Have the American Spirit of Conquest. Thus you can successfully battle with and overcome difficulty.

7. Cultivate Personality. Personality is to a man what perfume is to a flower.

8. Help and Share With Others. The real test of business greatness lies in giving opportunity to others.

9. Be Democratic. Unless you feel right towards your fellow man you can never be a successful leader of men.

10. In All Things Do Your Best. The man who has done his best has done everything. The man who has done less than his best has done nothing.—*Chas. M. Schwab.*

You will find the key to success under the alarm clock.—*Franklin.*

THE ROAD TO SUCCESS

Starts whenever a boy and God meet,
Is never made short by crooked work,
Is no man's private driveway;
Was never laid out by an idler;
Is litered with discarded conceit.
Has only one trail-marker—"Keep to the Right,"
Is frequently infested with mud-slingers.
—*Clinton W. Lee Company.*

"Some folks fall into fortune; but nobody ever yet fell into success."

The great high road of human welfare lies along the highway of stedfast well-doing; and they who are the most persistent, and work in the truest spirit, will invariably be the most sucessful; success treads on the heels of every right effort.
—*Smiles.*

"Would you succeed? Then toil to transfer the bone from your head to your back."

SUCCESS

It's the coward who quits to misfortune,
  It's the knave who changes each day,
It's the fool who wins half the battle,
  Then throws all his chances away.
There is little in life but labor,
  And the morning may find that a dream;
Success is the bride of endeavor,
  And luck but a meteor's gleam.
The time to succeed is when others,
  Discouraged, show traces of tire;
The battle is won in the home stretch,
  And won 'twixt the flag and the wire.

—*Service.*

SUFFERING

Though he were a Son, yet learned he obedience by the things which he suffered.

—*Hebrews* 5:8.

Hammering hardens steel but plays havoc with putty. Which are you?

Who ne'er has suffered, he has lived but half.
　Who never failed, he never strove or sought.
Who never wept is stranger to a laugh,
　And he who never doubted never thought.
　　　　　　　　　　—Rev. J. B. Goode.

For what glory is it, if, when ye be buffeted for
your faults, ye shall take it patiently? but if, when
ye do well, and suffer for it, ye take it patiently,
this is acceptable with God.

For even hereunto were ye called; because Christ
also suffered for us, leaving us an example, that
ye should follow his steps.—1 *Peter* 2:20, 21.

WHY MEN SUFFER

At the Pool Bethesda sat a poor cripple who
had suffered as an invalid for 38 years.

Jesus had compassion and healed him. Meeting
him in the temple later he said: "Behold thou
are made whole. Sin no more lest a worse thing
come to thee."

Does this give us the key to why the 38 years
of suffering? Probably also to some of our own?
　　　　　　　　　　—E. L. M.

THOUGHT

___

Thought takes a man out of servitude into freedom.—*Emerson.*

WHY NOT THINK?

___

It's a little thing to do,
  Just to think,
Anyone, no matter who,
  Ought to think,
Take a little Time each day
From the minutes thrown away,
Spare it from your work or play,
  Stop and think.
You will find that those who fail
  Do not think.
Half the trouble that we see,
  Trouble brewed for you and me
Probably would never be
  If we'd think!
            —*Author Unknown.*

As a man thinketh in his heart, so is he
            —*Proverbs* 23:7.

THINKING

If you think you are beaten you are.
  If you think you dare not, you don't.
If you would like to win, but think you can't,
  It's almost a cinch you won't.
If you think you'll lose, you're lost,
  For out in the world you'll find
Success begins with a fellow's WILL.
  It's all in the state of mind.
Full many a race is lost
  Ere even a step is run,
And many a coward fails,
  Ere even his work is begun.
Think big and your deeds will grow,
  Think small, and you'll fall behind;
Think that you can, and you will—
  It's all in the state of mind.
If you think you're outclassed, you are,
  You've got to think high to rise.
You've got to be sure of yourself before
  You can ever win a prize.
Life's battles don't always go
  To the stronger or faster man,
For sooner or later the man who wins
  Is the fellow who thinks he can.
                              —*Walter D. Wintle.*

Keep the telephone of your mind forever transmitting thoughts of love, purity and joy; then when selfishness, lust and hate try to call up, they get the busy signal. After awhile they will forget your number.—*Selected.*

Carelessness and failure are twins.

If you have half an hour to spare, don't spend it with someone who hasn't.

When in a fix, sweating will get you farther than swearing.

Let mules do the kicking.

Honking your horn doesn't help so much as steering wisely.

Notice that two-thirds of "promotion" consists of "motion."

Defeat is often a spur to victory.—*The Y. Men.*

Thought, a power which binds or makes men free
The precedent of actions yet to be.
A guide, a builder of self-control
Shaping the destiny of the soul.

—*Amy Baker.*

"The soul is dyed with the color of its leisure thoughts."

YOUR MENTAL GARDEN

Resentment is an ugly thing,
　It crowds the roses out;
Keep your mental garden fair,
　Put harmful things to rout.

Seed-thoughts that you cultivate
　Within your fertile mind,
Bring forth varied blossoms
　According to their kind.

Anger, malice, worry, fear,
　Are noxious mental seeds;
Quickly rid your mind of them
　Before they choke as weeds.

Faith, gentleness, humility,
　Truth, patience, selfless love,
Are specimens of seedlings rare,
　Approved of God above.

Your mental garden is a place
　In which you daily dwell;
Let nothing ugly flourish there,
　Safeguard and tend it well.
　　　　　　　—*Grenville Kleiser.*

You live with your thoughts—so be careful what
they are.—*Eva Arrington.*

Each thought is a nail that is driven
   In structures that cannot decay;
And the mansion at last will be given
   To us as we build it each day.
                —George Eliot.

TRUTH

O say, what is truth? 'Tis the fairest gem
That the riches of worlds can produce.
                —John Jacques.

Look forth and tell me what they do
On Life's broad field. Oh, still they fight,
The false forever with the true—
The wrong forever with the right.
And still God's faithful ones, as men
Who holds a fortress strong and high
Cry out in confidence again,
And find a comfort in the cry:
"Hammer away, ye hostile hands,
Your hammers break, God's anvil stands."
                —Samuel V. Cole.

Truth is the knowledge of things as they are,
and as they were, and as they are to come.
                —D. & C. 93:24.

Take your stand boldly upon Truth, and tho error assail you upon a thousand sides you need fear no man.—*Grenville Kleiser*.

Truth is the beginning of every good thing, both in heaven and on earth; and he who would be blessed and happy should be from the first, a partaker of truth.—*Plato*.

TRUTH

Truth's the beauty we see
In deed sublime and free,
When the mind is serene
And the heart, fine and clean.

Truth's the beauty we feel
When the heart throb is real,
And thought is lifted high
Above star fretted sky.

Truth's the beauty we know
When our souls are aglow,
With the seraphic fire
That evokes muse and lyre.
—*Nephi Jensen*.

VALUES OF LIFE

Supposing today were your last on earth;
  The last mile of the journey you've trod;
After all your struggles how much are you
      worth?
  How much can you take home to God?

Don't count as possessions your silver or gold;
  For tomorrow you leave them behind;
And all that is yours to have and to hold,
  Are the blessings you've given mankind.

Just what have you done as you journeyed
      along;
  That was really and truly worth while?
Do you think your good deeds would offset the
      wrong?
  Could you look o'er your life with a smile?

We are only supposing, but if it were real,
  And you invoiced your deeds since your birth;
And you figured the "profits" you've made in
      life's deal;
  How much are you really worth?

  —*Anonymous.*

A GENTLEMAN'S CREED

He does not seek the wealth of the world,
    Nor prestige, nor power, nor fame.
He does not ask for honors to grace
    The plainness of his name.

His life is rich with priceless gems
    When Truth and Faith applaud,
When friends can look at him and say,
    "He has won the trust of God."
              —Remelda Nielsen Gibson.

We lose the peace of years when we seek the rapture of moments.—*Bulwer Lytton.*

THE BEATITUDES

Blessed are the poor in spirit; for theirs is the kingdom of heaven.

Blessed are they that mourn: for they shall be comforted.

Blessed are the meek: for they shall inherit the earth.

Blessed are they which do hunger and thirst after righteousness: for they shall be filled.

Blessed are the merciful: for they shall obtain mercy.

Blessed are the pure in heart: for they shall see God.

Blessed are the peacemakers: for they shall be called the children of God.

Blessed are they which are persecuted for righteousness' sake: for theirs is the kingdom of heaven.

Blessed are ye, when men shall revile you, and persecute you, and shall say all manner of evil against you falsely, for my sake.

Rejoice, and be exceeding glad: for great is your reward in heaven: for so persecuted they the prophets which were before you.—*Matthew* 5:3-12.

VIRTUE

Virtue and vice are both prophets; the first of certain good; the second, of pain or else of repentance.—*R. Venning.*

Say to your soul, "Let no unclean thing enter here."—*Dr. Maeser.*

Let virtue garnish thy thoughts unceasingly; then shall thy confidence wax strong in the presence of God; and the doctrine of the priesthood shall distil upon thy soul as the dews from heaven.

The Holy Ghost shall be thy constant companion, and thy scepter an unchanging scepter of righteousness and truth; and thy dominion, shall be an everlasting dominion, and without compulsory means it shall flow unto thee forever and ever.—*D. & C.* 121:45, 46.

"Virtue is its own reward."

"Be not deceived: God is not mocked: For whatsoever a man soweth that shall he also reap. He that soweth to the flesh shall of the flesh reap corruption: He that soweth to the spirit shall of the spirit reap life everlasting."—*St. Paul.*

The body, overcharged with excess, weighs down the mind together with itself and fixes to the earth that particle of the Divine Spirit.
—*Horace.*

Lust when it is cherished, bringeth forth sin; and sin when it is cherished, bringeth forth death.
—*St. James.*

The vulgar story is Sin's frivolous comedy. For those whom this vile amusement enthralls he later stages his sad and dismal tragedies.

—*Leo J. Muir.*

To dread no eye and to suspect no tongue is the greatest prerogative of innocence; and exemption granted only to invariable virtue.—*Johnson.*

The contemplation of celestial things will make a man speak and think more sublimely and magnificently when he descends to human affairs.

—*Cicero.*

The end of life is to be like God, and the soul following God will be like Him.—*Socrates.*

WILL

Aim for a goal, then start on your way,
It may take a year, or only a day.
Travel slowly, and watch for mistakes—
Don't worry about the time it takes.
The path may be rough and mostly uphill;
But you'll get to the top by using your will.

—*Waldo G. Cook.*

The quality of a man's life is dependent upon his strength of will to accept or reject the issues of life, not as he wants them to be, but as they are.
—*Paul A. Anderson.*

People do not lack strength; they lack will.
—*Victor Hugo.*

WORK

There is not a creature, from England's king
    To the peasant that delves the soil,
That knows half the pleasures the seasons bring,
    If he have not his share of toil.—*Anonymous.*

Getting a vision and not living by it is like a sprouting seed that does not get above the surface but is withered by the very sun which awakened it.—*Unknown.*

Being forced to work, and forced to do your best, will breed in you temperance and self-control, diligence and strength of will, cheerfulness and content, and a hundred virtues which the idle will never know.—*Kingsley.*

BE STRONG

Be strong!
We are not here to play—to dream, to drift.
We have hard work to do and loads to lift.
Shun not the struggle, face it: 'tis God's gift.

Be strong!
Say not the days are evil. Who's to blame?
And fold the hands and acquiesce,—O shame!
Stand up, speak out, and bravely, in God's
          name.

Be strong!
It matters not how deep entrenched the wrong,
How hard the battle goes, the day how long;
Faint not,—fight on! To-morrow comes the
          song.   —*Maltbie D. Babcock.*

"No one rides dead-head on the road to happiness—if you reach that goal, you must pay your
fare."

Nothing is more fun than to have a little more
to do than you can get through with.
                              —*William Wrighley.*

Thou shalt not be idle; for he that is idle shall not eat the bread nor wear the garments of the laborer.—*D. & C.* 42:42.

The ruin of most men dates from idle moments.—*Hilliard.*

"It is in following the course of least resistance that men and rivers go crooked."

"Open the cocoon and you destroy the butterfly."

"Each pleasure that comes to us free from effort and free from responsibility turns into misery in our hands."

When men are rightly occupied, their amusement grows out of their work, as the color petals out of a fruitful flower; when they are faithfully helpful and compassionate all their emotions are steady, deep, perpetual and vivifying to the soul as is the natural pulse to the body.—*John Ruskin.*

The pots of gold at the rainbow's end
Are sought by the teeming mob;
But the fairies who guard them choose as their
friend
The man who loves his job.—*Anonymous.*

How much easier our work would be if we put forth as much effort trying to improve the quality of it as most of us do trying to find excuses for not properly attending to it.

—*George W. Ballinger.*

WORRY

No man ever sank under the burden of the day. It is when tomorrow's burden is added to the burden of today that the weight is more than a man can bear. Never load yourselves so. If you find yourselves so loaded, at least remember this: It is your doing, not God's. He begs you to leave the future to Him, and mind the present.

—*George MacDonald.*

Finish each day, and be done with it. You have done what you could. Some blunders and absurdities no doubt crept in; forget them as soon as you can. Tomorrow is a new day; begin it well and serenely, and with too high a spirit to be cumbered with your old nonesense.—*Emerson.*

I HAVE FOUND TODAY

I've shut the door on yesterday,
  Its sorrows and mistakes;
I've locked within its gloomy walls
  Past failures and heartaches.
And now I throw the key away
  To seek another room,
And furnish it with hope and smiles.
  And every springtime bloom.

No thought shall enter this abode
  That has a hint of pain,
And worry, malice and distrust
  Shall never therein reign.
I'll shut the door on Yesterday
  And throw the key away—
Tomorrow holds no doubts for me,
  Since I have found Today.

—Author Unknown.

"Worry is a state of spiritual corrosion."

It is not work that kills men; it is worry. Work is healthy; you can hardly put more upon man than he can bear. Worry is rust upon the blade.

—Henry Ward Beecher.

BITS OF WISDOM

The most profitless thing to manufacture is excuses.—*B. C. Forbes.*

"The man who persistently appeals to the best side of his fellows is rarely disappointed."

The world is blessed most by men who do things, and not by those who merely talk about them.—*James Oliver.*

"Priestcraft is holding a church position for the money there is in it."

"Look for no reward for goodness, but goodness itself."

All things have been done in the wisdom of him who knoweth all things.—*II Nephi* 2:24.

"If the world despises you because you do not follow its ways, pay no heed to it. But be sure your way is right."

"O God, that any one should put an enemy in their mouth to steal away their brains.
            —*Shakespeare.*

"Give whatever countenance and help you can to every movement and institution that is working for good."

Dost thou love life? Then do not squander time for that is the stuff life is made of.
                                        —*Franklin.*

Knowledge if stored away and not put into use may corrode in time.—*Eva Arrington.*

My business is not to remake myself, but to make the absolute best of what God made.
                                        —*Robert Browning.*

The highest and most lofty trees have the most reason to dread the thunder.—*Charles Rollin.*

"It is easier to gather up a bag of loose feathers than to round up or head off a single lie."

"Some people depend too little on the Lord, and some people depend too much on Him."

Gratitude expressed to others is a balm of sweetness that makes life more pleasant.
                                        —*Eva Arrington.*

"When you're in the right you can afford to keep your temper and when you're in the wrong you can't afford to lose it."

Lost! Somewhere between sunrise and sunset, two golden hours, each set with sixty diamond minutes. No reward is offered, for they are gone forever.—*Horace Mann.*

"Examine yourself each night and see if you have progressed in knowledge, sympathy and helpfulness during the day."

"True liberty consists in the privilege of enjoying our own rights, not in the destruction of the rights of others."

Though we may be learned by the help of another's knowledge, we can never be wise but by our own experience.—*Montaigne.*

Real glory springs from the silent conquest of ourselves.—*James Thompson.*

"The consciousness of duty performed gives us music at midnight."

"There are two things we should learn to forget —the good we have done to others and the evil others have done to us."

There is only one failure in life possible, and that is not to be true to the best one knows.
                                        —*George Eliot.*

Men are always invoking justice; yet it is justice which should make them tremble.

—Mme Swetchine.

"If you don't want to do something for some one else Christianity hasn't done any thing for you."

The first and best victory is to conquer self; to be conquered by self is of all things the most shameful and vile.—*Plato.*

Reputation is a bubble which a man bursts when he tries to blow it himself.

Pure self-denial is our good angel's hand bearring the gates of sin.—*Abbe Mullois.*

Truth is the strong thing. Let man's life be true!—*Robert Browning.*

This is a world of action, and not for moping and droning in.—*Dickens.*

Have a purpose in life . . . and having it, throw such strength of mind and muscle into thy work as has been given thee.—*Carlyle.*

Carry religion into common life, and your life will be rendered useful as well as noble.

—John Caird.